ARE YOU RACIST?

Root Causes Of Racism that Nobody Talks About

JADA ALEESHA

Introduction

We were sold the idea that Racism is evil, and Racists are evil. The purpose of this sale is to allow the buyers and the sellers to believe that they are better people than the Racists are, to believe that racists are these few unknown creatures that rarely ever surface on the planes of society.

These beliefs were easily fed to us with the help of the media and various platforms that seek to turn racism into this foreign concept that only exists for a few people.

We, as human beings, would love to believe that we are separate from the people and things that are bad, unacceptable and monovalent. When we can consciously separate from these things, it makes us believe that we are good people, and the evil only exists outside, somewhere in some forbidden land where the sun never shines.

We feel ashamed for not being 100% wholesome, loving beings, twenty-four sevens. This came from organized belief systems supported by religious doctrines and deriving from fundamental concepts that said certain traits mean that we are corrupt and, therefore, unacceptable and unlovable people.

One of the main reasons why we cannot understand the system of racism is because we cannot understand other people, why they behave the way they do and why they possess unique characteristics.

We do not understand each other, and we do not understand ourselves. This is because we do not take the time to observe our own thoughts; therefore, our focus remains on others.

We divert our focus unto others to avoid those negative, hidden, unconscious aspects of ourselves that we not only desperately want to avoid, but are also in super deep denial about. We want to desperately believe that we are super benevolent beings that are never capable of hating or hurting anyone. We have to believe this; otherwise, we are those repulsive, malignant, unlovable rejects of God.

**"We cannot solve our problems with the same
thinking that created them"**
(Albert Einstein)

We assume that solving racism only involves the accountability of the "Perpetrator"; yet, in today's world, this approach has not yet brought any sense of promise to a solution. This is telling us that there has to be more energy invested by more people to reach any kind of agreement where this issue of racism is concerned. Blaming victims for the crime is never beneficial or positive. However, the victims can truly play a role in an ongoing and recurring problem that negatively affects them.

We give the victims a pass because they are the victims, but this mentality and way of being are hurting them than helping them. We live in a universe that operates in a particular way, one that gives us more of whatever we are and keeps us wherever we are. It is super important that the victims are supported, nurtured and understood; however, the path to a solution may be harsh and seem unfair, but sometimes this is how the victims will learn from their mistakes and ultimately liberate themselves.

~~~~*

What is awesome about this book is that it is actually offering real solutions; solutions that may seem simple. However, sometimes the things we believe will work are the things that are adding to the problem and the "little" things that seem irrelevant are the things that hold the highest potential.

The approach to start solving racism in this book may seem simple but consider these things....

* Why wouldn't you be happy that the work that has to be done is somewhat simple or easy?

* We are at a desperate point in our life path where we should be open to try anything, even just to see, what will work. We should be testing everything that we could, as I believe that we do not have a great amount of time.

You might have come across books in the past about racism; maybe some of them were offering solutions, but for the most part, these solutions are some of the same old, redundant, counter-productive methods that people still expect to work even after seeing that these actions for solutions are not really bringing lasting results.

This book is about showing people how to solve a global problem by addressing the root, suggesting that we have to stop expecting an outside system to have the answers because we have the answers within ourselves.

"ARE YOU RACIST?" is a "how to solve racism" book, even if the first few chapters aren't giving you this idea; keep going, you'll get there eventually.

Do not make the mistake of jumping straight to the solutions chapter; if you do this, you will not totally understand why I chose the methods and techniques that I did.

"ARE YOU RACIST" is an easy read, as some of the insights and philosophies will be familiar to you, while others are quite fresh and groundbreaking, which also makes this book one of the most interesting books ever written.

IMPORTANT THEME OF THIS BOOK

Every action we take first exist in our minds. Our subconscious mind and thoughts influence us much more than the conscious mind. Our subconscious is what is driving our actions.

We can only heal the major political problems of the world by addressing them from a "subconscious mind level.

The Politics didn't start with politics, they started with each individual's mind and emotions.

Jada Aleesha

CONTENTS

Disclaimer

In this book, there is the use of the word "trigger". I used this word in the context that it was initially used, that in which a Psychologist may use it. This suggests that there are things and occurrences in our lives that irritate or re-irritate subconscious/ dormant trauma and emotions within our being.

I decided to keep this word in this book because I believe it perfectly describes the conditions in which I am referencing.

I started writing this book before the insensitive people in our society turned the word "trigger" into something ugly.

~~~~*

If you happen to encounter a tone of pessimism in this book, just remember there is a chapter called "Solutions."

CHAPTER 1

The Creation of a Racist Mind

There are things we like and dislike about everything around us. Even the things we love and cherish, we tend to find different parts of them that we deem as inadequate or weak. We do this with our personalities, bodies, genetics, gender, talents, careers, our partners, etc. Therefore, of course, we also apply this to the Race and Ethnicity to which we belong.

There will be traits that come with our race that we love, like or just accept. Then there will be those traits that we reject. The things we love and accept about ourselves are mostly predicated upon the validation we received as children from our parents. The things we reject about ourselves are usually those that were also judged and rejected by the Caretakers in our childhoods.

Most if not all of our emotional issues can be linked to something that happened or didn't happen in our childhood. Our minds are so fragile within the first few years after birth that we are so easily affected and influenced by all that is happening around us. A child's emotional system is just as delicate as its new-born body.

When our parents reject aspects of who we are as children, our fragile emotional systems will be hurt by this rejection; it then personalizes the hurt and now rejects it in the self. The child's mind learns that "since my parents rejected these things, I must reject these things to get approval from my parents and approval in general". The child will also reject these things in other people.

Our parents rejected and shunned the things about ourselves that they saw as bad behaviors, they teach and program us to reject and condemn anything that the society labels as immoral actions and "inferior," unacceptable attributes.

We will hate these traits in other people because they will remind us of the things about ourselves that were rejected and also the things we don't want for ourselves because they were taught to be bad by societal standards.

We will also condemn these attributes when we see it in individuals or in groups including religious groups, social groups, gender, and race.

We were all conditioned to believe that certain characteristics are acceptable, and some aren't. We resist these traits in others as a way of rejecting them in ourselves to feel stronger and more secure or what we want to believe is security.

Let it be known that, hate, and in this case, racial hate has very little to do with race itself. Human beings use race (racism) to generate a sense of superiority to feel better about their own race and or the self in general. Hate has more to do with the hater than the hated. The hater hates the race of people whom he believes embodies the things he hates about himself and the things he doesn't want for himself.

This all means that the hater (in this case, the racist) is suffering. There is much suffering involved with being hated, especially if this hatred is being backed up by an aggressive kind of oppression. But what we fail to recognize is that the hater is living in deep emotional pain and suffering and sometimes even more than the people he oppresses.

One of the main reasons why it's hard for the races to connect with each other right now is because most people have not discovered that people on both the giving and the receiving end of racism are suffering from tremendous pain.

The height of hatred and bigotry within the hater's mind indicates his level of pain and suffering.

Pain from our childhood results in us needing power and significance; most people didn't learn how to positively work with their pain, so they project it outwards in a negative way. There is not one person who is not carrying some amount of pain and trauma from their childhood. Some people have more pain than others.

Most of the times, our pain is suppressed and the beliefs and thoughts behind the pain become subconscious. The energy that comes with the emotions associated with this pain gets trapped in the body and are mostly surfaced and expressed because of an outside influence that caused a trigger.

This means that people become bigots, antagonists, and racist criminals because of wounded parts of themselves that they try to deal with by means of hurting others. When it comes to racism, the saying of, "hurt people, hurt people" have never been more valid.

When we are unhappy with certain aspects of our lives and who we are, the easiest way for us to deal with our pain is to project it and direct it unto others. This gives us a temporary emotional relief.

In this reality, we live largely through the Ego's perspective. We are constantly scanning our surroundings to find anyone or anything that is "different," then we view the differences, as not just differences but inferiorities. We then interact with or treat that person or thing as such.

Let's take a closer look at how this works:

Young White male (let's call him Jesse), is growing up in a home where his father emphasizes the importance of manliness and what it means to be a strong man.

Jesse sometimes feels rejected by his father. This feeling of rejection came as a result of the father causing Jesse to feel as though he is not "man enough", son for him.

Their home had very subtle and covert racism within it that Jesse would consciously interpret as everything, but racism. He receives direct and indirect, negative subconscious messages about people of other cultures, languages, sexuality, gender, and race.

His parents would like to believe that they are doing a pretty good job of raising their son. After all, being super politically correct is the right way of training your son and defining his worth solely by his masculinity is good and normal.

They were deeply moral people, who were highly revered and respected for advocating for Civil rights and Political Correctness.

Jesse goes into the society, like all of us trying to fit in. Fitting in usually entails the necessary requirements that may or may not be in line with what makes us good enough for whichever group we want to fit into. This forces him to measure himself next to everything and everyone.

A son feeling rejected by his father since a tender age, carries within his body, the energies and emotions of disapproval and exclusion. In order for Jesse to maintain a sense of "good self-perception" for his identity, he goes around sizing up everyone according to the "decent, good enough person" requirements.

Jesse does this because he recognizes those things in people that he hates about himself as well as the things about people he does not want for himself.

This is Jesse's way of forming preferences for what he desires as a fitting image for himself and his potential group.

In other words, this is being done for him to know who he is, who he wants to be and who and what he wants to identify with and as.

From knowing what he wants, he will move towards it and become it, and then everyone outside of him and his group will become different and separate from him. The people who are different from him serve as objects of his judgment and condemnation. This is a mental process for his mind to soothe itself of the deep emotional pain he is carrying from his childhood.

Jesse now judges, excludes and in a passive way, verbally attacks anyone whom he believes does not have, want or exude any of what he and his group, deem as valuable, worthy or "cool."

Jesse's personality is one of those that are not overly aggressive when expressing negative opinions but can be occasionally. Just like a bully, he attacks others based on being different. He interprets differences as inferiorities.

His beliefs of what constitutes one's worthlessness mirrors his own feelings of inadequacy. This creates a strong force within his being that must release itself. He releases this energy by aggressively or passive-aggressively judging and attacking.

He attacks people on anything that makes them different, like gender, age, looks, sexuality, personality, religion, culture, and race. This gives him a temporary relief from the pain of feeling less of a man. The very pain that remained inside of him that was derived from the way his father felt about him.

He turned out to be one of those people who are extremely angry at the world. He would be highly critical of others and express it in very passive ways around "civilized" people, because remember he, like most of us, had upbringings where our elders sought to do "the right thing" from being politically correct.

 His Parents were overly expressive of the moral importance of being kind and nice to people who are different, because they considered themselves to be decent, civilized citizens of modern society. But this didn't prevent Jesse from becoming a passive/aggressive racist.

Trying to be politically correct as a parent will only work in reverse. Children are much more discerning than we realize. The double message that is being sent in a home that is covertly racist but also is politically correct will be understood and received by the child's subconscious mind.

Therefore, Jessie received the message that being a non-white is not as good as being white, while not feeling man enough for his father. To feel better about his manhood, he sometimes verbally degrades non-white people.

His racist attitudes are more related to his feelings of powerlessness. His racist feelings had more to do with him than the people he is racist towards. He uses his racism as one means to convince himself that he is powerful, to compensate for feeling less than strong. He looks down on someone's race to feel better about his masculinity (or the perceived lack of).

People will look down on someone's race to feel stronger in general, it does not have to be related to masculinity, it could be any part of their lives that they believe they are lacking in. This demonstrates my earlier point that hatred has more to do with the hater than the hated. This is the development of the racist mind.

Earlier I mentioned that people tend to interpret and mistake differences as inferiorities. As it pertains to race, if an individual is looking for someone to feel superior to, instead of seeing race or skin color as just differences, they will view it as a flaw or an inferiority.

You only have a need to feel superior due to existing feelings of inferiority. You will only want to be above because you feel "below."

We may see or hear of aggressive racial pride. This is not true pride, it's actually shame disguised as pride. If a White nationalist is proud to be white and declares it to the world, most of the time it is a way of concealing some shame related to his whiteness and or some other aspect of himself. The abrasive and obnoxious declaration of white pride and black degradation is to emotionally cope with his "self's" frustration by convincing himself and others that white is superior.

Any person with this mindset will view the differences in others as a threat and if these differences are a threat, then it will become a competition. Since it's a threat and competition then they must degrade it and lessen its value to condition themselves to consciously believe that it is not a competition and to get the potential competitors to believe in their own sense of inferiority.

~~~~*

You may find it easy to come down with judgment on people like Jesse but try to think long and hard about your own upbringings, was it that different? We all belong to and identify with a race, we all grew up in environments that were, to some degree, aware of racial politics. We all seek to deal with our deep-rooted pains by projecting them outwards. We all seek validation for ourselves by means of seeing aspects of ourselves as better than others.

Every dark quality that exists in an individual also exists within you. From the most notorious mass murderer to a child who lies to get his way. The root of these characteristics comes from an energy source that every living being has inside of them. Some beings choose to allow the pathology to take over to the point where they act out aggressively while others seem to be more in touch or in tune with the light side of who they are.

The degree of inner pain, will determine the degree of suffering we will inflict on others.

CHAPTER 2

What is Racism?

Would we all agree that Racism is defined differently by different sources? I've observed that Racism means different things to different individuals and different groups.

Racism: Cambridge.org/dictionary

Noun [u]

/rei.sizm/

The belief that people's qualities are influenced by their race and that the members of other races are not as good as the members of your own, or the resulting unfair treatment of members of other races:

- My definition(s):

1. Discrimination, abuse, antagonism, unfair treatment, hate or resentment of a race of beings because of a system's perceived notions that they are inferior, by genetics and/or less valuable based on character and/or behavior.

2. People's racial differences being the basis for separation and exclusion.

3. Anti-Blackness.

4. The -isms of Race

~~~~*

The belief that people's qualities and characteristics are influenced by their race is neither correct nor incorrect. It is a generalization, yet it is not a total lie.

This kind of generalization seeks to de-humanize people and further creates separation among races. However, there are certain existing qualities and characteristics that are influenced by people's genetics, as well as their culture, norms and common interests.

This is because they have grouped together by identity and created belief systems, which further generated more common beliefs and, thus, a similar reality for the whole group.

A system of racism usually has a dominant side, which can be supported by institutions like Governments or just scattered self-interest groups throughout the land, whose objective is to enforce the idea of separatism, control and the destruction of another race.

Throughout history, we have seen different unfortunate events that were racially motivated; these shape and mold our present perceptions of the human virtues and moral standing.

There are beliefs supporting the idea that we humans are civil, selfless beings with sprinklings of a few immoral and ruthless individuals. There is also the notion that most people cannot be trusted, "as we can see on the news every day that the overall human condition is soiled and spoiled by decadence, evil and immorality".

Now, when it comes to the topic of race/racism, these perceptions are equally distributed among people. While some individuals believe racism is gone or has been significantly reduced compared to a certain time in the past, some members of society believe that large numbers of people are interested in the oppression and destruction of another race or races.

Considering present day and the number of events that included racial crimes, I believe most people have at least a slight understanding that the belief of a non-racist society was highly flawed.

Recent events have been unfortunate, but they have served as a revelation for humanity at large. It was both a curse and a blessing in a sense, as individuals have suffered and died, but it was also an awakening for those who were in denial.

People lived in denial for years regarding racism, because denial puts them in a safe emotional place. People were in denial, so much, that different races would be around each other with a tight uncomfortable tension and ignore it as if it's not there. There were awkward moments where each individual would be aware of the truth but behave clueless in each other's presence just appear civil. It's amazing how many people are in denial, yet these very people who exist within their own minds. The very minds that think different degrees of racist and prejudice thoughts.

Which means most people are out of touch with their minds and emotions.

In the past, laws were passed against the blatant discrimination and attacks on "minorities." Some laws were also removed to ensure freedom and integration between white people and black people. People subsequently spent years evaluating the policies of the past and also their behaviors and beliefs.

Eventually, people began to feel guilty and ashamed because their evaluations of the past made them seem inhumane and uncivilized by today's standards. People took time to reflect on their old ways and became somewhat more conscious of their behaviors and attitudes towards others.

In my opinion, this is about the only good thing that enforcing laws against hate crimes and discrimination has done. As far as racism itself, and the factors that drive it, the root and essence of racism are still very much alive. I may argue that it is here just as much as it always was, only in a different form.

<u>Who are the real racists?</u>

There is not one human on this earth that doesn't belong to one of the races. Even if there was one such person, we could assume that this person belongs to the "one-man race." His race would still be a race by itself.

We all identify with a race. Even the people who claim that they don't, still do. To say "I don't identify with a race", is to indirectly identify with a race. You are acknowledging that race exists by not identifying with one; this means, on some small level, you recognize your racial position in society, where you can identify or not identify with it. This is a form of indirect racial identification.

To say, "I don't see race," is to acknowledge that there is "race" to see, which means you see race. To say, "Race does not exist," is to confirm the concept of race, which means you believe that race exists.

I am making these statements to say that most times, when people say these things, it is not necessarily true for them. The intention may be good, but it is not actually what they truly believe. These are the things people want to believe or what they wish they could believe. These are things that people say because they believe it's right, but not because this where they actually are.

Being that we all, in some shape or form, identify with a race, we dissociate ("dis-identify") with other races. You cannot claim a group without separating yourself from the ones you don't identify with.

Once this identification process begins, you will inevitably form ideas, thoughts and beliefs about the other groups, based on what makes them good or bad and different or the same as you. This is the pre-judging level of racism; in other words, this is how/where prejudice begins.

You will not be able to look at anything or anyone that you believe is separate or different from you, without processing some negative and positive things that you know about them.

To see someone and judge them as different or separate from you is the first level of prejudice. Bigger prejudice and racist thoughts and beliefs grow from this basis.

What I'm ultimately saying here is that WE ARE ALL PREJUDICED and WE ARE ALL RACIST.

<u>"How can Black people be racist if we are not in the social, economic position to be racist?" Here's how:</u>
The "powerless" position that blacks are in, creates the desire to be in the opposite position of total power. (This desire is stronger for some black people than others). The desire for power, holds within it, similar feelings and beliefs of the people who are actually in the position of power (i.e. White people).

This means that black people also have the racist thoughts and emotions that white people feel from being in the position of power, but in a different capacity and to a different extent. So, black people's racist feelings are currently existing; they just are not able to put the intentions of these feelings into systematic operation because they do not have the social, political power to do so.

As far as I'm concerned, if Black people are experiencing the feelings that come with the desire to be in "power", then yes, Black people are racist. It's just that the power aspect of their racism is in a state of potential, because there is always a possibility for the power roles to switch in our society.

"If this power role should switch, would this mean that whites will automatically stop being racist?" Of course not, because the thought, beliefs and feelings that they had while being in power, would still be inside of them. This is the actual state that blacks are in right now.

~~~~*

<u>Who should hate who?</u>

Some people believe that being a victim of racism automatically puts them in a position of the incapability of being racist. They believe it's fair and justified to resent or hate someone who has hurt them and so, their hate should be understood, expected and accepted.

It is understandable that they believe their feelings are justified. Just about anyone can relate. We've have all dealt with someone who had treated us unfairly or was abusive in some way, and at some point, in time. It's expected that our feelings towards them would not be positive.

While this is understandable, it is important that we understand that being racist cannot be determined by people's social-political position in history or present day; but rather the feeling/mental state itself, the negative feelings themselves and the mindset itself.

If we could set aside what we believe is justified, how the resentments were created or what brought us there, we could easily open your minds to view racism as a much broader concept.

If you keep pointing to someone else as being the only one with that unique racist trait, you won't be able to heal because you will always see these people as the ones who need the healing, while keeping them responsible for your situation and pain. This also causes you to be blinded to any change needed on your part. This also keeps the society stuck in these negative social political cycles because there cannot be any thorough healing for a positive change.

It will take effort from all sides to recognize and acknowledge their responsibility in creating a better reality. It would not be called racism if only one race was involved.

Whether you are the perpetrator or the victim, your negative racial feelings are racist. The victimization has brought you to this dark existing state. This state of being is negative and related to race, so it's a racist state and you too are racist. It doesn't matter how you got there, the reality is that you are there and you are what you are.

It's easy for one to say, "I'm not racist because I didn't do anything to them; they did something to me, I should hate them and not the other way around." This view suggests that the perpetrator or hater has no reason to hate the victim, and only the victim has good reason to hate. I understand this kind of thinking; however, there is a deeper psychology to this.

The mind doesn't need a physical forceful attack or invasion for it to feel attacked or invaded.

A single race believes they are right to resent another group because they were treated unfairly and abused for an extended period. They have a hard time understanding the motivations for the hatred directed towards them. They don't understand the reasons for it or if there is a reason; as a result, they view it as just hate that stems from hate, assuming, "There is no reason for them to hate us."

It's time for us to understand that there is no such thing as "no reason". There is nothing that happens and there is nothing that people do, that is done for "no reason" or is pointless.

This mindset stems from a very limited outlook in this life. This limited outlook stems from the mental state of valuing all that is physical over what is mental and emotional.

If human beings should learn the simplest forms of delving into their subconscious aspects, it will be easier to: 1. Relate to other people's "evil" and 2. See that we all do good and bad things at different degrees. We would see that hatred is something we all feel, and we don't always need "big" reasons like slavery, war or abuse to hate. We wouldn't be stuck on the belief of "they have no reason to hate us."

All people hate, sometimes for very shallow or seemingly shallow reasons; for example, some people hate others for being poor. Some people hate because of a person's bad attitude. Some people are hated because of an occupation they chose, like being an exotic dancer.

Let's not forget the people who hate because of differences in political beliefs, traditions, culture, norms etc.

In these situations, the haters aren't actually being abused, pillaged, enslaved or having war waged against them, yet they hate.

Whether big or small, hate exists and when dealing with the issue of racism; we should make the priority about the hatred itself, and the root of what's driving it, not necessarily the perceived invalidity of it.

Let's not support the idea that the only racists are the aggressors or the people who have been the aggressors throughout history.

Even the "hated" hates and they too hate for very "empty" reasons. It's just hard for people to recognize that they are hateful when they are at the receiving end of the antagonism. They are so focused on the negativity directed towards them, that they miss any opportunity for self-analysis or introspection.

They are also consumed in the egotistical need to be the ones who are good and right. This is when the victims take on a very humble exterior to "make believe" that they are not capable of "bad actions" as the obvious perpetrators are.

There is always a reason for everything we do and feel and our feelings are always valid.

The idea of hating for no reason is empty. It is sometimes explained as "people hate what they don't understand." While this explanation is not as empty, it is not bringing much profound understanding to why people hate.

Our hatred is never just that. Hatred is deeply rooted in a galore of subconscious energy that is associated with fear, insecurity, weakness and resistance.

Hate is just a surface emotion, expressed to disguise the weakness as strength and "hardness." Hatred is the output of aggression from having a certain weak point triggered. You can never have a strong negative reaction to anything if there wasn't a trigger and there would not be a trigger if there wasn't existing "root fear".

That fear gets triggered whenever a person sees or thinks about the object of their hatred. The existing fear that is there gets activated and erupts, then projects into anger or rage, which may take the form of antagonism and degradation.

The mind perceives the person it hates as an invasion on its comfort, safety, status and sense of power.

The mind is a system that allows our thoughts to alert us to any potential threat. Something doesn't have to be physically dangerous for it to be a threat. In fact, anything that gives or causes negative feelings for us is a threat for the mind.

This feeling of being attacked will exist in any person who has high levels of intolerance within them. This is both the victim and the perpetrator. This further explains that it's our existing beliefs, feelings and emotions that make us prejudiced and racist and not necessarily our social/political position in society.

<u>Who can be racist?</u>

I heard some "pro-black" interest groups, defining racism as simply, "White Supremacy," suggesting that only those people who are either white, identify as white and/or benefit from white skin privilege, can be racist. They believe that people in the black community are not in the social/political position to be racist, as they suffered at the hands of white supremacy.

The people who are at the receiving end of racism, not only acquire a resistance towards their haters, but also a disdain and rejection of the people in their own groups. The resistance towards their haters is accepted because it is expected, due to the abuse suffered at the hands of the "haters" throughout history and present day.

The disdain for their "own" people derives from their internalized feelings. This is when the hated starts to hate his reflection because it reminds him of why he is hated.

A strong need for mainstream acceptance sends him in the direction of adapting to the requirements of the mainstream ideals, after which he carries a scorn for those in his race or community who have not conformed.

So not only are the "victims" capable of racism, but they harbor much more resentment because they send it in more than one direction.

The process that I just described can be referred to as Racism; even though it is more self-directed, it still pertains to the subject of race.

The people who support the idea that "Racism is White supremacy", believe that people of darker skin tones cannot be racist because they are at the victim end of racism, and they don't benefit from white supremacy, as it tends to loosely include even those who aren't European-Caucasian, but possess whiter or lighter skin.

However, let's go deeper.

For hundreds of years (and possibly thousands), there has always been favor given to people of lighter complexions. The concept of white supremacy is rooted in the belief that people of whiter skin belong to or are coming from a superior lineage. The whiter, the better, and the closer you get to white in appearance, the more acceptance you will get by the majority of beings who benefit from or "conform" to this belief system.

Human beings prioritize acceptance. Most (if not all) people want acceptance by all. When people feel excluded, they feel unwanted, thus, have a need to feel wanted and included.

Darker skinned races on the planet have suffered deeply for centuries, from this process of not being accepted. Even their "own" people of dark skin tones are "un-accepting" of dark skin tones.

Ego needs to be in a safe place, and this may take the form of self-rejection and a simultaneous gravitation towards what is accepted.

This process does not only apply to race. People in general want to be widely and openly accepted; if not, they inflict the hatred unto themselves then reject the people who remind them of those unacceptable, unlovable aspects of themselves.

You cannot hate or resist anything without desiring something else. So, if dark people are rejecting their own skin color, it means that there is a desire for whiteness or "non-blackness."   This is an involuntary and unconscious subscription to a certain aspect of white supremacy.

Now there would not be a desire for whiteness without an existing belief that white is better. This would suggest that people have bought into "whiteness" as the standard and being better than "non-whiteness."

Both whites and non-whites live by this ideal. All People are influenced by white supremacy in this way even the people who claim that they are not, which means that it is debatable that all people from all races are White Supremacists to an extent.

This further supports my point that if racism (by the "Pro-black Interest Group's definition) is, in fact, "white supremacy", then everyone, including dark-skinned people, are racists.

Of course, most people would dismiss this idea out of shame, guilt and/or just not being self-aware enough to observe the workings of their subconscious minds and the opposing truth within it.

Some may argue that hatred for one's own race or color is not racism but simply, "self-hatred". While they are correct that there is some self-hatred involved, they are missing the point that it's actually both racism and self-hatred.

One is driving the other. Racism projected outwards or within one's own race is derived from some of the same kinds of emotional processes. They are both dealing with the same issue, both pertaining to race and the many intricacies within them. It's all "Race"-"ism". The -isms of Race.

If you call it color-ism or shade-ism, I can still refer to it as racism, because color and shade is a strong part of the concept of race.

Not only can all types of racial affairs be considered racism, but they affect all races. Most people probably would not agree or even fathom how it could be true that even white people suffer in this system of racism.

The people on the receiving end of oppression, discrimination and abuse are in pain for sure; however, it takes considerable amounts of pain and hurt to inflict oppression, discrimination and abuse unto others.

The longer it takes to awaken to the fact that all people suffer emotionally with racism, the longer the pain of racism with linger and even heighten. This is because in addition to being ignorant to the suffering of those on the giving end, we continue to blame and shame them for the evils of the past and present.

Should We Disprove Stereotypes?

People's entitlement relative to their own racial backgrounds is coming from years of being programmed that their ethnic genetics or skin color makes them superior and therefore more deserving.

The entitlement is further fueled by their observation of other races exuding or demonstrating certain behaviors, traits, and features that are seen as undesirable or unacceptable.

These behaviors get attributed to a particular group when they are done over and over by members of that same group. These are what we call stereotypes.

It's not possible to live in a diverse society as this one and not have racial stereotypes. So many different factors influence certain behaviors of a race of people, their culture, their genetics, their social-political position in society, their religious beliefs, customs, traditions, norms etc. These things make races, nations, and ethnicities unique and different from each other.

When people become used to their own norms, culture, and traditions, it's hard for them to accept other people's. Some of these differences may give rise to judgment from all sides. This is sure to happen as the ego is constantly looking for a reason to separate the "self" from others. The ego views the cultural differences and norms as inadequacies or the opposite depending on the social/economic position of the viewer.

The viewer wants to believe that the differences mean that something is wrong with a person from another group because it makes him feel more stable and normal and therefore superior. For example, if a Caucasian person believes that Black people are violent; this makes that Caucasian feel less violent and therefore better than Blacks.

Some people believe that an effective way to resolve racism is to prove stereotypes to be "un-true" or inaccurate. They believe that if members of outside races get to see more atypical examples of any race or group, then that will help to reduce some of the fear that leads to people finding that race or group threatening.

Atypical examples of a race can help to reduce some of the anxiety that produces more racist feelings within people, but it will never be the answer to all of what will bring strong resolutions to racial politics.

Stereotypes are just a fraction of the whole of what keeps racism alive. Stereotypes being true or not, are not the biggest part of what keeps people from accepting each other. It is what the stereotypes represent for them personally and subconsciously.

When we see people of other races, we automatically stereotype them. We are doing this sometimes without notice. Stereotyping is the ego's way of maintaining the "I am different" perspective. "If someone's race possesses some negative attributes that makes him or her different from my race, then my race get to be good and therefore superior". The ego is needing of this process to keep its fears covered.

Stereotypes are a part of the basis of which racial disdain stands. People see members of a certain race and the stereotypical images appear in their minds. Then there is this tension and the need to escape the tension.

Escaping the scene means, escaping the uncomfortable feelings that were brought on by the thoughts of those stereotypical images.

People do this to avoid the reflection of themselves in those stereotypes. It is a reflection because if you fear something, then the fear is a part of you. You don't have to be the exact image of the stereotype for it to be your reflection.

For example, if you grew up being in fear of poverty from believing that being poor is disgusting and pathetic, when you see someone from a certain racial background that is usually associated with poverty, the subconscious fear of being poor or feeling poor is now triggered. The poor people are a reflection of your fear of being poor, or maybe the part of your mind that feels poor.

Another example:

There are groups/races of people that have a stereotype of being rich and sophisticated. You may feel anxious around these types of people. This anxiety is not just based on the rich people's economic status. Instead, it is coming from your self-conscious feeling of being "less than" compared to these types of people.

Then you try to avoid these people to escape the pain and the fear of feeling less than. These "classy" people are a reflection of your fears.

We see now that proving stereotypes wrong won't be the total solution to prejudice and racism. We have to delve deeper into the subconscious mind to identify the underlying reasons for our fears and anxiety towards stereotypes.

~~~~*

If these typical behaviors are considered wrong, immoral, or ruthless, then the people who exhibit these actions will be condemned, which leads to them being discriminated against and treated badly.

Stereotypes are actually true because members of particular groups continuing to do similar things and take similar actions. But of course, there will be some exceptions to the rule. Even though some actions and attributes may be true for some or even most, it will not be true for all.

This is common sense. We can all find many exceptions to the general perceptions of people in different groups, yet some folks choose to hold on to the generalizations because it serves an egotistical purpose for them.

The Human ego thrives on knowing that it has an opportunity to be superior to others. In this case, it's related to the belief that, "if the people who look a similar way has undesirable qualities, that they all share, then it makes them inferior which makes me superior".

So not only do people hold on to the belief of the existence of other people's stereotypes but they also desperately need to.

People choosing to open their minds to the idea that no one group of people are all the same, will not bring significant healing, as far as racism goes. In fact, most people already know that every race or culture has exceptions, yet they still hang on to these beliefs.

Now let's say that it is true that all people of a race were the same. What would be the problem here? Why would people being the same in the group they identify with, become a problem for the others?

Most stereotypes are true, but the fact that people get anxious, angry and irritated around the people they believe embodies certain typical attributes, should show us that the problem is not the existence of the stereotypes by themselves. It's actually the negative thoughts and beliefs, related to people's own pain (and how the stereotype affects their self-concepts) that gets triggered when they are around the "stereotype."

It's ok to look at stereotypes and try to understand them, what they mean and why people's culture influences their personalities, but the work cannot end there. People need to know that true healing occurs when we venture in. What we feel exist within us, so that's where we need to go.

Finding what aspects of ourselves are being triggered when we encounter the people who embody "the stereotypical behaviors" will be the source for reducing the fears and anxiety that creates bigotry and tension between the races.

Grey.B.VVV   *~~*~~*

You are trying to disprove stereotypes to prove your worth to the people who look down on you. This tells them that you are afraid of them and their opinions of you, so much so, that you'll alter yourself (and your people) to please them. The need to disprove stereotypes, tells others that they are your superiors. ∿∿∿

Anti-Blackness

One of my personal definitions for racism is "Anti-blackness."

To say that racism is anti-blackness, is to say that black people are the only people who are hated? This is not what I am actually implying.

Blacks are definitely the most hated of all the groups but there is a layered structure to racism. A hierarchy, which has white people at the top and black people at the very bottom.

The people who are non-white and non-black, fall right between whites and blacks, above blacks but below whites.

Now, Anti-blackness is the same thing as pro-whiteness, so the people between blacks and whites are hated less than blacks but they are also loved less than whites because they are "blacker" than whites.

"Blacker", meaning, not black but "melanated". Its high levels of melanin that causes blackness/ darkness of the skin so anyone who has more melanin than whites can be referred to as "blacker" and having "blackness".

So, this is why I can personally define racism as "Anti-blackness" (which does not describe a reality where blacks are the only people that are hated but means that the darker/blacker you are, the more you will be hated.

We are all racist? How so?

Most people would disagree with my opinion that all human beings are racist.

They don't understand how this could be.

What we need to understand is, people can be racist, but have different intentions.

We all have a dark side and a light side, a conscious mind and a subconscious mind. We are both good and bad. (Some people have a bigger dark side than light side).

We can suppress or hide our racist feelings within our subconscious minds (dark side), while still being mostly influenced by our light side.

So, when it comes to the subject of racism, some people have bad intentions, some people have good intentions and others may be more neutral.

Most people in this society see the overt, "ill-intentioned" or antagonistic racists as the only racists. Most people see the people who are nice people as non-racists. However, because someone is racist, it doesn't mean they are bad, evil or want to discriminate or antagonize. Some people have more love in them than others, so these people display less racism than others but is still racist nonetheless.

In my opinion, all people are racist. It's the intention behind our racist feelings that makes us dangerous or not dangerous racists.

Some people will always have a problem with my view that all people are racist; if you are one of these people, please read below. Please read below even if you are not one of these people.

How to recognize your Racism

1. If you feel any shift or change within your emotional system when you see people of other races.
2. If you have a preference for "your own kind".
3. If you have a preference for races of people outside of your race.
4. If you judge people of other races relative to anything racial.
5. If you feel like you have to be nice to other races.
6. If you feel like you have to be nicer to the people within your own race.
7. If you identify with a race. (which we all do)

These points might seem ridiculous but hear me out for a while.

A huge problem with racism in this society is that we have been selling it as an abomination for a very long time. This is because most humans have not awakened to what racism really is. We view racism as we view most so-called sins, i.e. evil and diabolical.

Religion and law have turned most emotions and emotional states into crimes and sin, so we can't see that our racist feelings are emotional states that came about as an automatic response to the politics of diversity in our environment.

Having racist feelings in this life is a natural process of the mind. It is negative, but not evil, sinful or wrong (or right).

When people separate from each other because of identity, the mind develops preferences and then creates both negative and positive perceptions of both the people it prefers and the people it does not prefer. Moreover, this is an aspect of what helps to create the racist mind. This is a negative emotional process; this is not an evil process, which means we cannot and should not continue to treat racism and being racist as "the worse things in the world."

This is what we have been doing for decades and we cannot afford it anymore because it continues to create a whole host of problems, which I will speak on, later in this book.

Society says being racist is wrong, so people deny being racist. I say racism is not "a wrong", so you shouldn't deny it. (You'll understand later, keep reading).

CHAPTER 3

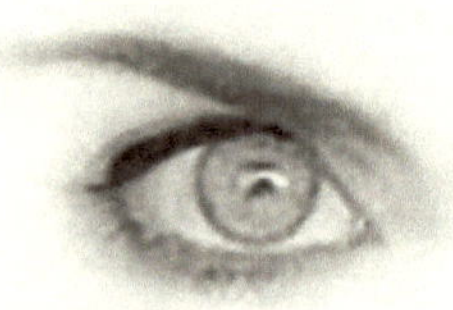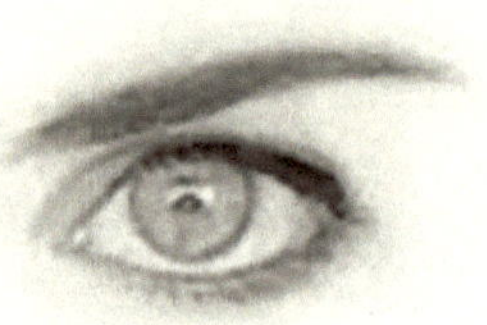

The Look of Power

People already separate themselves from each other using identity, which is supported by their preconceived notions of each other. The differences in our look are what initiate these notions.

It may seem absurd or out of touch to say that people base their prejudice on looks but let me inform you that a great deal of our scorn for others are coming from the way they look.

When it comes to racism, we like to center our focus on all the big or seemingly big issues around it, like discrimination, segregation, slavery, police brutality, white privilege etc. However, these things exist because of us separating ourselves from each other because of the difference in our looks.

A definite way to confirm someone's race is by looking at him or her. A blind person will only care about race if he knows or was trained to detect it by voice, accent, or some intuitive ability. Unfortunately, when it comes to race, most people aren't blind.

In this physical world, "the look" or "a look" has a super strong influence on our general life views. We use "the look" to form just about eighty percent of our opinions, perceptions, and decisions about everything. "The look" is used to determine or remind us of what and how our conduct should be.

How many times have we heard this from people? "Don't do it", "don't do that, it's not a good look," or "we do things this way because it looks right."

We base everything on looks. At the root of our social norms and politics is the need to look right and to look like we are good. People will totally disregard their feelings and comfort for the right look. We want to look politically correct, We want to look morally right, We want to look physically good, We try our best to up-keep with whatever the "right look" entails. No wonder we try to get away from whatever we believe doesn't "look" right or good.

People associate certain cultures and races with things like poverty, degeneracy, mediocrity, and even ugliness. They know this by looking at it. (It becomes a "look"). Therefore, they aspire to create the opposite of these things.

From people acknowledging that they don't want a certain (look) image for themselves, they decide (unconsciously) that the look they desire should be the standard and a vital element of, the dominant society. This is what I refer to as "THE LOOK OF POWER." The concept and the making of a dominant society involves "The Look of Power" and a huge part of this ideal has a racial element to it.

Throughout history, the concept of a "dominant culture" has been the source of what people would base their aspirations on. It sets the standards for, and influence education, government, morals, religion, Arts, traditions, norms, success and even beauty. For example, in this society, the beauty standards takes a more European form and so does most other standards that we live by.

The dominant society ensures that its members are equipped with most of what is required. This means that to fit in, you have to "look" the part.

In this society and for a long time, white/Caucasian has been "The Look of Power." Power looked like this; the closer you get to the look, the more privileged you will be and so, the more privileged you will feel.

From the outside looking in, it seemed that those people with the European features would be able to have access to the things that were almost unattainable to others.

Throughout history, Europeans have managed to develop and maintain power and hegemony over the rest. There are theories as to how it all started but what gave them that spark to start? What made them believe in their own sense of entitlement this much? What or who gave Whites that confidence.

Whatever it may be, the "look of Power" has been a means for its "longevity."

The interest in complete and total power is the catalyst for implementing all types of strategies to keep the concept of a "white" look of power as the dominant society. This may have been a sinister plan, used in Psychological warfare for non-Europeans to "internalize" the process and as a result, become and expect less.

This means, the person who is born and raised in an environment where the people who have all wealth and power don't look like him, will develop very low expectations and will settle for the second or last place.

On the other side of this, the people who look the part will try their best to keep up with the requirements of the ideals of the dominant society, which are the images, the conducts, the appearance, the morals, the values etc. They already have high levels of confidence that their "look" gives to them, therefore, there is a very strong desire and interest to reserve a stable position in this (mainstream) society.

This will also come with the rejection for those outside of this dominant community and for those who chose to not conform.

It is not possible for this rejection to exist without it being noticed. People's disgust for others usually shows, even when they are trying hard to disguise it. It is noticeable.

When the people who are being rejected notice the rejection and the disdain, they become bothered and sometimes outraged. Some may become very rebellious and even disorderly which result in even more rejection and disgust from the powerful ones, which create more separation between the communities.

In our world, the white "mainstream" society find some of the minority groups as chaotic, immoral, and anarchical which the mainstream perceives to be unacceptable conduct.

The minority groups view the mainstream as uptight, withdrawn and "stand-off-ish" which comes off as unsociable and unapproachable.

Now the physical appearance (look) of the people in each community is expected to always match these typical attitudes, demeanor, and conduct. Each side recognizes the look when they see it and the separation continues.

~~~~*

The look of power also has an inherent system of hierarchy. This is based in ethnicity, color and even gender plays a part in how racial groups are categorized and ranked on this ladder.

Again, the most obvious way to recognize people's identity is by the way they look. The color of your skin is one (look) factor that determines where you will be on the racial hierarchy. The whiter or lighter you are, the higher you will be and the darker your skin is the lower you will be placed.

The issue of race is a hierarchical system within itself, and this system is inherently "colorist."

In some ways, the racial hierarchy and the color hierarchy is the same but sometimes they are two different things because some races have different shades of the same people. For example, there are Asians who are white skinned and there are some who are brown.

Now, what about the people in the dominantly white/light skinned races who aren't white/light skinned? They usually are the poorest and disadvantaged of the group, while most of the times living in the same countries. This, of course, causes a disconnection and segregation among the people of the country.

In almost every case where some people are more impoverished than the rest. There is always an angry disposition of the ones who are less fortunate. It's stemming from the "less fortunate" seeing their reality as unfair and unjust. They usually become very aggressive, rebellious, and sometimes lawless. The people within the upper class are generally extremely judgmental towards these less fortunate people. So certainly, this reinforces the notion that darker people are naturally ruthless hooligans and white/light skinned people are always the clean, decent, law-abiding citizens.

One reason why the darker people are more aggressive and rebellious is because many of them believe that there are systematic forces working against them. They see white and a light-skinned dominant society as a representation of a deeper hidden shadow operation, that exist to ensure that they fail. They become even more bitter and therefore more rebellious which causes a strong tension between both worlds. Both sides attribute their unique actions and attitudes to "a look" (dark skin/white skin) and now it becomes a situation of " the people, who look like that, act like this."

The people who look a particular way expect certain behaviors. The folks who "look" poor, unkempt, rough, dark/black represent the "violent" lower class. The ones who look presentable, clean, expensive, whiter/lighter represents "THE LOOK OF POWER."

How big is the "look"?

I had mentioned earlier that the look of power also includes those whom are considered beautiful (attractive). I used the word "beauty" to pull your attention to the truth of it, as most people are "somewhat", subconsciously aware of this. It's one of those things that we notice but never really speak about which brings up an even more silent belief, that physical attractiveness is a small, insignificant part of our lives. This is the biggest lie ever told. In fact, beauty is not only an important aspect of our lives, but it also affects the social, political, economic aspects of the society. Beauty is also playing an important role in the fundamentals of our overall happiness, well-being, and spiritual evolution.

What does this have to do with "THE LOOK OF POWER"?

For centuries, the nations on Earth have been working on their social/economical advancements. A large part of this advancement is success.

Success is said to be "Money + Power = Respect." Whoever invented this line, forgot to add to the equation, the sum of beauty.

Most people are only subconsciously aware that beauty and success go hand in hand. Whether they are speaking of physical beauty or non-physical, as far as I'm concerned, beauty is one of the root layers to the purpose of our aspirations. This means that everything we are doing is to create beauty.

We want to build a strong economy to create a beautiful living environment and to experience the "beautiful" feeling it brings. We go to school to feel the beauty of graduating, not to mention the beauty of the success that we believe it will bring. We enter relationships to experience the beauty of love, desire, and intimacy. We want nice things because they are beautiful and bring beautiful feelings. This has no limits. Everything we do is to live in the beauty of the experience. We are trying to create mental, emotional, or physical beauty.

"For many people, there is much "beauty" with having power but most of these very people are not soundly aware of the power in beauty."

There is a certain unspoken potency to being beautiful or attractive. People know about this, but these people don't seem to be aware of just how deep it runs.

When we deal with aesthetics and physical beauty, we mainly think of things like the potential lovers we can attract, the compliments it can bring us and that "it's a nice gift from God." We rarely ever take the concept of beauty to a higher philosophical realm. We don't take time to view the bigger peripherals surrounding the "small" topic of beauty. We are not seeing how far it goes and everything it extends to and leads to.

Aesthetics among many other things in this life is trivialized. It is viewed as a small, empty, superficial subject for the "shallow" and frivolous. This is because we exist in a predominantly "left-brained" oriented world where both men and women are programmed to have a very narrow way of thinking.

Whatever made us this way, is to be debated. In the meantime, this is where we are, and this kind of thinking affects all aspects of our lives.

The left side of the brain is also the male brain. It views things in a strict, linear logical order. It is not open for alternative possibilities. This all means that when it comes to politics, people on earth are mostly able to see how the political issues are affecting political issues and not how the seemingly small, "irrelevant" things affect the bigger things. With this particular issue, most people are not observing how beauty affects the political arenas.

How political is the "look"?

We all use the words look/looks and beauty interchangeably or the word looks in reference to a kind of beauty or the lack of. Whatever is pleasing to the eye, is the "look" we gravitate towards and aspire for. And depending on how emotionally weak we are, sometimes we try to get away from it.

Regardless of how extremely narrow-minded we are, with a little help, we can easily make the connection of how beauty/looks extend to even governmental politics.

Take, for example, a location like Brazil. Brazil has the potential to improve and build a decent economy with help from the tourism sector of their government. This is so because hundreds to thousands of people are intrigued by Brazil because of the popular belief that the people are very "easy on the eyes."

Another example is certain kind of jobs are reserved for attractive people like a news Anchor or an airline hostess. Let's not forget the fact that rich and powerful men usually go after really attractive women. It subconsciously tells the men at the "bottom" that they will never be able to get a certain type of woman unless they are filthy rich, and it tells the women at the "bottom" that they don't stand a chance if they don't look a certain way. This becomes political because these people at the "bottom" will become reluctant and not aspire for more if they believe they don't stand a chance.

Therefore, we can argue that beauty can give individuals the confidence or the drive to aim for more and likewise cause others to settle for less because of the belief that my current "beauty" status limits my ability to attract the kind of people and success I want for building a better life.

Whether this concept seems far-fetched or not, no one can deny that one reason we all want to become successful, is to attract a particular type of people in our lives.

How "racial" is the "look"?

You are either blind or in denial, if you aren't aware of the racial element of beauty/looks in our society.

European features have always been adored, praised, and envied. THE LOOK OF POWER is a package of the right race, color, status, and wealth and yes, beauty.

In later years, having at least one of these qualities could invite you in the "dominant society's" "power circle" but it was not always like this. Only some decades ago, white people, and black people in America were segregated and opportunities seemed super bleak for those who weren't white. Even if a black person had money, (which is one main ingredient for entering the upper-class power circles) he would still be seen as unequal to mainstream America.

A black person with money and or fame would probably be treated better than the "average negro" but he wouldn't be fully embraced and welcomed within the dominant culture. In today's world, the laws are different, so people learn to "act" differently.

In today's world, if you have one of the requirements for success, this could work in your favor but having more than one will easier rent you a space among the rich and affluent.

The "right" color and or features are automatic grounds for acceptance. This is one reason why the people who don't fit the ideal for the look of power is so frustrated and angry all the time because acceptance is one of the most primal needs for human beings. Some may hide this need with "cover expressions" like pride or arrogance but what they really want is to be accepted.

The look of power is the look of success and the look of success includes beauty. The idea that aesthetics plays a part in people's perception of success is a lost concept, i.e. people aren't consciously aware that they use beauty to place value on human life.

Whether it's about beauty itself or the color of skin or someone's ethnic features, we are still dealing with a look. We look at people to know what they are. Whatever they look like "ethnic wise" and or beauty wise, can determine the level of acceptance they will receive from people.

Being accepted in the power circle means having the "right color", the "right" race, the "right" money, the "right" features (beauty). This is why even though being Caucasian is number one the list there are others who fit in because the color aspect, can include non-whites who have white/light skin e.g. Asians, Latinos, some Indians, and "Arabs," mixed race people who are light and even black people who are light.

The race aspect and the color aspect are highly related but not exact because there are white people who are deeply tanned but still white.

The right money can get anyone through the door regardless of race, color, or looks. There may be some limitations socially, but "still".

The "right" features could mean anyone from any or color as long as they meet the "attractive" criteria, especially for women. This is where it gets really interesting because no matter what race or color you belong to, the features that are considered attractive is still European "like." A very dark-skinned woman will be "attractive" because they have features that are closer to the standard. For instance, a black person of African descent, with very dark skin can be considered beautiful because they may have a straighter nose or thinner lips or just because they have a look that is atypical for their race/ethnicity; this is how the racial hierarchy is created because what we don't realize is, the racial hierarchy and the beauty hierarchy is one and same.

This might seem inaccurate, as there are people who, (for example) are white but not attractive. Well, there is a deeper aspect to be understood here.

Perceivably, whiteness and beauty have always been paralleled. The truth that is not being told is that subconsciously, white people see themselves as superior because of this. We overlook this because we were taught to believe that what we actually value in ourselves and others are "much bigger things", like our strengths, accomplishments, moral standing etc. So, because we've been convincing ourselves of this partial lie, we miss the truth that we really value more superficial things like skin color and the idea that color can make one more beautiful and therefore more valuable.

This concept of a racial/beauty hierarchy creates, lead to, or worsen the self-hatred in many "ethnic" communities and all the direct and indirect problems that come from that kind of self-hatred. It's also a big part of what is creating classism, in society. The whitest, richest attractive people in the highest classes and the darkest, poorest, "ugliest" stays in the lower class.

Earlier, I said more than once, that most people tend to interpret differences as inferiorities. I also pointed out that we use our visual capacity as our strongest source for judging and defining others. So, when non-blacks see black people they form a belief that these people must be inferior based on just how very different they look.

The fact that people in between the black community and the white community, (the "browns") either have fairer skin and or straighter hair, they are somewhere higher than blacks on the racial/beauty hierarchy yet still lower than whites.

With whites being at the top, the people below develop this desire to become more like whites. Even if whites at one point were abusing them, that desire still exists in them because people, in general, will aspire for whatever they see as more powerful.

Author's perspective

For those who are having doubts that beauty helps to shape your feelings towards the human value. Take me for example. I am a Black female and there are times I go out among people of all different backgrounds. I observe the way they treat me as a black person when I'm dressed attractive and look pretty versus other times when I don't try to look beautiful. It's almost as if when I'm pretty, I'm not black anymore. Not white but something else, something acceptable, adored, and easily welcomed among the classy and rich.

It's like this: White skin is beauty, but beauty is beauty and beauty is the look of power and the look of power is success and success give you value and so you are accepted.

When it comes to "The look of Power, which is one of the stronger concept that drives racism, black people suffers the most, emotionally. There are other non-white races that suffer from the politics of different aspects of the look of power like "colorism" or "shade-ism" and other aspects of racism however, the people of African descent has the most distinct features of all the races. The largest population of the darkest skins, the hair is course, and the typical facial features are the furthest from the "European ideal".

The "Browns" may feel inferior to white people but sometimes these very brown folks carry a strong disdain towards blacks. This is because when one feels inferior to something, he tries to find something else to feel superior to.

It's not possible to believe you are superior to someone without showing it in some form or another. So Black people are faced with discrimination and sometimes abuse from not only Caucasians but also pretty much everyone who isn't black.

The word "look" is not only related to the superficial sense of the word but also the understanding that a certain "look" comes with specific stereotypical behaviors.

I believe one main factor that initiated racism towards blacks was their look. I believe the fears from black people's stereotypes came about after the initial construct of racism in the "western" world came to be.

The common misconception is that racism has nothing to do with superficial "looks" and more relating to "the behaviors about the people who look like that."

However, think about one thing. In history, when Black people were still in Africa, they didn't always act in most of the stereotypical manner like they do now in America, yet they were still hated, to the point where they were chosen to be the slaves. This means the initial reasons for the hatred towards them was not based on stereotypical behaviors or so-called character flaws.

Most of the "bad actions" and "misconducts," derived from a non-conformist, rebellious stance that some black people took on because of being mistreated, abused, excluded and marginalized. Slavery itself created so many psychological maladies that further created the dysfunction that lead to what we know today as " bad stereotypical behaviors." These stereotypical behaviors may have helped to heighten the fear and anxiety that came with the "black look" but this is not the initial basis from where the hatred for Black people stems from.

Most people might be confused regarding the idea that white supremacy is based on looks or beauty but even the theory of black people being less evolved than others was mostly based on the physicality of the African human, who were considered at one time to be only three fifths of a Human being.

Some people say that the issue stems from non-blacks not accepting what is different or that "people hate what they don't understand." However, in order for people to know what is different, they first have to see it and for people to "hate what they don't understand," they first have to see it then decide if it is understood or not understood.

Society may have an even bigger disagreement that beauty is playing a role in people's racial preferences. It will be hard for them to grasp this concept because they've replaced the truth with the lie they want to believe because they are ashamed of it. They are ashamed that they are vain and shallow, so they lie to themselves for such a long time, that the truth got lost and the focus got diverted unto a false reality.

The lie is that white supremacy is based on something big and political rather than something "small" and shallow (looks/beauty).

This is like something in your life that you're ashamed of, so you've convinced yourself of the lie you want to believe instead. You suppress the truth for so long, that the lie becomes true after a while.

It's amazing how fixated we are on superficiality and how much time we spend on trying to look good and how intrigued we are by things like beauty pageants, yet we have not followed beauty to its most political grounds.

I understand that it's hard to see how a huge issue such as racism can boil down to looks because for centuries, us as a society would drown the root factors of every political matter by surrounding them with topics, other issues, and words that are related but does not point to the source. This creates a false representation of what could be a simple truth.

A broader look at the "look"

All human beings on Earth are influenced by the beauty standard as it is. Some people live in deep denial about this. The reason for this denial is that non-white people, especially blacks, were taught that it is wrong to reject any part of their heritage and that they are "sell outs" and traitors if they do. Being a "traitor" or "sellout" comes with the price or penalty of being bashed, shunned or rejected by the community.

This caused black people to suppress the truth that they too, have an inherent appreciation for Eurocentric beauty more so than Afrocentric beauty. Just like the truth about "looks" in racism, it gets hidden and pushed down because of shame and is replaced with something else that is more acceptable.

So black people feel ashamed about who they are, what they prefer, and then being shamed by the people in their own community for not embracing their "God-given" beauty. This is enough to make anyone hide and suppress their true feelings.

In the black community, the response to the present beauty ideals is expressed in different ways. There are those black people who openly and actively reject this beauty ideal, there are those who feel indifferent about it, and then there are the blacks who choose to be honest and forward about embracing societies standards for beauty. The "Afrocentrists" resent the fact that some black people have "conformed" and believe that these conformists need to heal themselves.

~~~~*

Being rejected and overlooked for having the wrong look, creates the desire for becoming the right look. Most people will not admit to it, others become non-conformists by rejecting it aggressively while trying to embrace the roots of their heritage.

I challenge people to question their reasons for this rejection, as they may find that there is much inauthenticity involved.

Some of these "Afrocentric" people, on an extremely subconscious level would also like to look like the " European ideal" and or have a partner who has these very features, but they are ashamed of it, so they disguise this shame with "declared" self-interest and Black pride.

Regardless of what you stand for, related to beauty, the truth remains that we are all impacted by the beauty standards and we all have an innate preference for it in some shape or form. Whether the preference is conscious or not, (willing or not) we naturally are espoused to this look as the "right look."

While we may argue that it is unfair, it is also unchangeable. People can change their minds about many things but when it comes to what they find to be appealing to their physical senses, (especially sight), they can't just choose to unlike it. We cannot just change our minds about what is pleasing to our tastes; this has never been done.

What can be done is, healing from the emotional, psychological damage and pain that occurred as a result of living and sharing space in a world where you aren't accepted. For this to happen people have to be willing to and honest to speak the truth on how they are really affected.

~~~~*

Placing value on beauty in its superficial form isn't wrong or right. Society may say its evil because we were all trained to believe that adoring material things makes us "ungodly" but even on a spiritual level, our collective intention is to create beauty for the Universe and ourselves. This means that our human purpose is to create beauty of all forms for ourselves and the universe at large.

Beauty can be used as another word for anything of our interests that is positive or desirable, which involves everything, everyone and all parts of our existence, physical and non-physical including thoughts, feelings, and concepts. Our life is all about creating beauty and the most beautiful version of every aspect of it. Even the systems that condemn the adoration of superficial beauty, exists because they support the idea of creating the "BEAUTY" of modesty, simplicity, and humility.

The problem is not superficiality in and of itself. The problem is people living with fears that causes them to devalue others because of their physical make-up.

One main factor that drives white racism is white people, not liking the "black look." They prefer the white look. It's easier for white people to accept those people who are in the category of non-black/nonwhite (also known as the "browns") because they have two or more features that may be similar to the European ideal. It's harder for them to accept the black look because it is most obviously different. The ego sees the differences as automatic grounds for separation and then comes competition.

~~~~*

The idea that "having black skin makes one inferior is not based on the color all by itself. Sure, the skin is black, but what about blackness that "oozes" inferiority to the mind? The answer is simple. Blackness as long been associated with negativity, evil, darkness, black is bad, black is sinister, black is scary, black is death, black is doom, black is depression, black is the devil, black is unpleasant, black is ugly.

Over time humans have attributed these labels to the color black, so when black is in human form (race), these stigmas still apply.

It is the "ugly" aspect of black, which people have attached to the Humans who are black. This has long caused a scorn, resistance, and rejection for black people because whatever people see as ugly they will reject. Then feelings that are even more negative arise and grow which lead to a social/political issue among black people and non-blacks especially Whites.

~~~~*

If you are still having an issue with this take on racism; if you are still finding it hard to merit the concept of beauty/looks influencing white supremacy. Well, the psychology works like this: " I am white, White = beauty, beauty = good, but I feel lacking in some other areas of my life.

You are black, Black = ugly, ugly = bad: Ugly is inferior to beauty, bad is inferior to good: you, being inferior to me means I feel superior to you and so I feel better about my "lacking."

Because most white people aren't consciously aware of this mental process, some of them (especially in earlier years) started to attach other negative beliefs to black people, like having a smaller brain, not being fully human, naturally less intelligent. Then these beliefs are magnified because of certain "typical behavior" that black people may have demonstrated along the way. These beliefs were created to build a more "concrete" and "meaningful" reason for black people's supposed inferiority because the real reasons had been made invisible and non-existent due to people's focus being directed to what seemed like more sensible and serious possibilities.

Grey.B VVV

May I add that even these "more concrete" beliefs came about because of assumptions about Black people's look. Meaning people believed that blacks were less intelligent or had a smaller brain because they saw the "negroid"/African features as being "Monkey-like". <<<<

Somewhere along the line, white people decided that their image should be the symbol of success. The people who have this look would find it easier to access success than others would i.e. education, opportunities, and money, power, respect, and yes beauty. Non-whites in general who accessed wealth and beauty became an extended part of the "THE LOOK OF POWER" but all in all, white skin remain a very potent element for success within the power circles.

The look of power and success, with all its requirements, including beauty, has helped to shape our perception of a human being's value, caliber and people's worth and right to life or death. Unbelievably, this is one of the psychological basis that drives the sinister systems and agendas that carry out acts like genocide, ethnic cleansing, slavery etc.

My take on this piece may seem like subjective philosophy but I see it as an unknown fact.

When people have uncomfortable feelings about another set of people, it is always stemming from excruciating emotional pain within themselves. Most times, they don't know that this pain is more self-related. They don't know how to escape the pain, so they will try to get rid of the people who they believe is causing their pain, instead of the pain itself.

Humans desperately hate the parts of themselves that they grew up believing is worthless. They also grew up believing that people who have these traits are inherently "worthless," like people who are dark in color, poor, ugly etc. The perceived worthlessness in other people reminds them of the perceived worthlessness in themselves. Hating, abusing or ridding the people who "embody" these so-called worthless traits is their mind's way of hating, abusing, or ridding themselves of these very traits. So really, they are just unconsciously fighting themselves.

~~~~*

We use physical appearance to identify and judge everything. We can only live by, operate, and function according to what is assumed from what we see or sense. Everything we perceive are objects of either our identification or "dis-association". They are here to remind us of different aspects of ourselves. They are either what we are, what we want or what we don't want.

People go after what they collectively find to be desirable, so anything that doesn't resonate as such will be rejected, cast out, and devalued.

This applies to all people, not just white people. It's hard for black people to see the truth in this because they remain at the receiving end. When people are at the victim end of anything, they will not want to see (let alone accept) the ways of their "enemy" or " oppressor" within themselves.

~~~~*

Grey B.g VVV

In this chapter, looks and beauty were suggested to be a central part of the psychological construct of racism. However, this is not the root layer of it all. Looks and beauty are just the physical representations of what connects to the deeper subconscious truth. If this doesn't make sense to you, let me shed some light on this "deeper subconscious truth." Here goes!

The reason why people aspire and seek out beauty and success are because they believe; this is how to get love. Likewise, people shun and reject ugliness, poverty, and weakness because they won't get love this way.

Aware of it or not, love is the most important thing for any living being and believe it or not, love is the most essential need. The physical essential needs that we know about, exist as a result of not feeling and having enough love energies in our bodies. (This is a truth and for some people a theory, that has its roots in metaphysics. Feel free to research it.)

∧∧∧∧∧∧

~~~~*

As far as I'm concerned, the two main ingredients involved with Racism is looks (THE LOOK OF POWER) and competition. It's so easy for people to use their sense of vision to identify and observe the differences between each other. Whenever there are obvious differences between people, the ego uses that as grounds for competition. If these obvious differences or an aspect of the differences is seen as unwanted or undesirable (looks), they become targets for attacks or bullying (and rejection); the attacker uses the things that makes the others undesirable to convince himself that "he is better and superior and so he has won the competition. (Where there are differences there is competition when the differences are considered undesirable, there is scorn).

~~~~*

Some people of today might have an issue with me saying, that the white look of power allows whites to succeed, as they may know countless people of color who have immeasurable amounts of success. I said this because this is the way it has been for a very long time, through-out history, however, I also mentioned that in today's society, money, color, and beauty does open doors for non-white people to enter in the high society circles among the white and powerful Money and or fame for non-white males; beauty, money, and or fame for non-white women.

This is actually a thing of the newer generations which some may believe to be a covert, strategic plan of a hidden white supremacist agenda, to operate and practice white supremacy under the guise of equality.

This belief of a hidden racist agenda is believable. Maybe on some high governmental level, there is such a conspiracy. Either way, the overt, historical "white" "look of power agenda has caused people of color to unconsciously and involuntarily hold themselves back from their own potential social and economic accomplishments.

Slow progress within non-white communities is a stagnant state that comes from the people's fear of "not making it" because of the color of their skins and or the way they look. Therefore, whether there is a grand conspiracy to hold back "people of color" from accessing wealth and power, the after-effects of the original overt agenda are still negatively affecting these people today.

What I previously described is one way in which what is known as **WHITE PRIVILEGE** works. White privilege, for the most part, is not a conscious process that involves white people strategically giving "their own kind" a pass. White privilege is a silent, subconscious, and unconscious reality that takes place in many different forms.

If white people are the majority and the most dominant in America and all people are prejudice to some degree, then you can bet that white people will be treated better by their own kind.

Most white people don't know that they are actually doing this because they have convinced themselves that they are not racist or prejudice. They may think they are being nice and try to be nice but the "niceness" comes across as very artificial. And sometimes the conscious effort to be nice can be seen as condescending.

The subconscious truth will show up in big and small ways, even as small as facial expressions. From black people's perspective, this is uncomfortable.

And even "little" things like facial expressions, reinforces the prejudice that causes black people and non-whites to feel a sense of "not belonging." And in turn, tells their minds that only whites belong. This sets a silent tone for our reality that says; "white people don't have to worry about having to encounter these uncomfortable situations. This within itself can be a privilege (at least compared to black people's reality).

What black people are calling white privilege is actually "the look of power" in full effect. It's simply white people going through life, having easier experiences because of their "white look", without even knowing it. This is one reason whites seem so oblivious to concept of White Privilege because if they've only lived from their white perspective, there is no other perspective to compare it to. So as far as they're' concerned, they don't have white privilege, they are just experiencing what is normal life for them, while black people experience a whole different life.

People of today like to question white privilege as a foreign concept. But I'm going to tell you that another term for white privilege is "Racism", (White Racism).

If you agree that racism exists, then you agree that white privilege exists.

The term "White Privilege" just simply describes how white people are least likely to be discriminated against because: 1. They are in the majority in the country and 2. They are the least hated. I challenge anyone to prove otherwise.

White privilege exists even in countries that are not majority white. Most non-white people tend to adore the white image, to the point where some of them will go out of their way to accommodate Caucasians even at the expense of "their own people."

Recently I heard of situations where some Asian countries have business places like nightclubs where black people aren't allowed but these very places have their doors fully opened for White people. Now, how is this, not PRIVILEGE?

When people say white privilege doesn't exist, they are neither wrong nor right.

There is no unseen force out there that provides specifically for white people or people with white skin. The universe (God) is not favoring whites over blacks. So, there is no privilege that exists for anyone eternally. However, down here on earth we have created a life where in history and present, the reality of hierarchy exists. And privilege does exist socially.

White people had perceived themselves as superior throughout history and this belief system has affected the different races negatively. This perception has traveled through generations and it still exists today in many subtle and hidden ways.

Whether white privilege is objectively real or real by perception, it is still real because whatever we are perceiving will be true for our minds.

CHAPTER 4

To

P

or

not to

C?

After the super dark ages of open racism, from slavery all the way into the 1960's and some parts of the 70's, laws were passed in America to release old policies. Old separatist laws were dropped and a new order for integration was put into place.

In this time and after, civic organizations and the government sought to create different ways to accommodate and include all citizens in social and political affairs. Black people, women, gays and other "minorities" wanted equality, rights, and justice from their government. While laws were passed to ensure rights and liberties, people were insistent on creating a society where all citizens became considerate of the sensibilities of the "minorities." This means that it wasn't ok to be outwardly expressive of negative feelings and beliefs about any "disadvantaged" group.

People weren't allowed to say or do anything overtly racist in public towards people of other races. This includes the usage of racial slurs and racial profiling.

POLITICAL CORRECTNESS IS BORN

Political correctness (PC) is a policy enforced by the "authorities" and the media to socially police people into avoiding expressions and behaviors that seek to verbally, emotionally or physically hurt or offend people who are/were disadvantaged.

The people who are/were marginalized and oppressed are the ones who are the most requiring of political correctness from others. For example, black people are more sensitive because they have suffered greatly at the hands of white supremacy, so non-blacks especially Caucasians are expected to be extremely careful and considerate of the feelings of "black folks."

In a world where people are super out of touch with what works effectively to actually bring true resolutions; it is understandable that this is the approach taken to deal with this kind of politics.

Political correctness isn't good or bad. The intention is to get people to do what's "right." So, we can say the initial intentions behind this policy were good, but because something is good morally, doesn't mean its effective. Political Correctness is in place to get things right but in my opinion, when it comes to matters like racism political correctness makes everything wrong.

~~~~*

Racism does not exist as a separate entity that can be monitored by rules, laws, and strict guidelines. Racism exists within people. This means that we are dealing with thoughts, beliefs, and emotions in relation to race.

We, in this life, are so out of touch with our own emotions that we are blind to the fact that political correctness cannot bring effective solutions. All it does is causes people to gloss over their true feelings and thoughts for the ones that are supposed to be "right." This further causes people to develop and carry shame about the truth, which causes them to suppress this truth, which results in a myriad of personal, social, and political problems, both small and big.

To truly understand more on this topic, we must understand some basics of how our minds and emotional systems really function.

~~~~*

Have you ever noticed that no matter what, you cannot get away from certain thought patterns and beliefs? Some of us developed beliefs since we were very young children and carried them into adult life and some people even grow old and die with the very negative beliefs from childhood. This is because whatever thoughts and beliefs we have created has a powerful response system in our bodies called emotions. Our emotions work as guidance to the nature of our thoughts. In other words, our emotions are our thoughts being played out in our bodies as sensations. Your thoughts, beliefs, and emotions are a real and true part of you as your fingers and eyes are. Not only are they a real part of you but they stay with you just as long as you keep them.

Your emotions are important, powerful nonphysical aspects of you, as well as your thoughts and beliefs. Your thoughts turn into emotions and over time these emotions continue to feed the thought which then remains in your system to grow into strong beliefs. These thoughts, beliefs, and emotions have a potent impact on your being that you cannot just separate or disconnect from. These thoughts, beliefs, and emotions become a part of us and help to shape our personalities into what it is today.

People cannot just choose to not believe or feel something. If you feel something you feel it, if you believe it you believe it. If you believe that worms are disgusting, you cannot just stop believing this. If you have a negative emotional response to worms being disgusting, you can't just end that feeling.

This psychological and emotional state applies to every aspect of our lives including the beliefs involving race and racism. People's original negative beliefs, prejudice, and sometimes bigotry that are related to race, still exist within them. Children adopt beliefs and attitudes from their parents and others. The feelings stay with them all through their lives. These feelings exist whether you are aware of them or not.

Political correctness shames people into suppressing their beliefs and emotions about everything political. It causes people silent themselves, hides the truth, and suppress it, while still being racist. These very people then go the extra mile to "politically correct check" and judge everyone who chooses to openly express the very things that they themselves are also thinking and believing. They know the truth and they know that we all know the truth but it's hard enough for human beings to admit the truth to themselves let alone the whole world.

Two people can know each other for years, sometimes sleep in the same bed and they will know that they have racist feelings towards people of other races but never admit it to their partner but instead continue to lie to each other, even though they both know the truth. This comes with a weird subtle tension that we all can sense but its deep subtleness makes it seems like it's not even there because it is deeply buried under a kind of "righteousness" that stems from shame.

Shame is one of the hardest emotions to identify. One reason is that it is most times stuck in the body from years and years of suppression. This causes the emotion of shame to be reluctant and sluggish. Number two is the fear of the truth and the shame that comes with the truth about the shame. There is a certain shame that comes with shame (or being ashamed), so people will deny the truth or even just avoid anything that could potentially show up the shame.

Humans have not yet experienced any healing from their racist feelings. Now we have a system and a society that uses political correctness and other counter-productive policies to silence and censor people. Going about life, this way only creates more problems for society because the unhealed emotional aspects of what breeds bigotry and separation are still existing and now people are being forced to not express the real and strong feelings that need to be released. This entire process causes people to become extremely angry and frustrated with feelings of being trapped mentally and emotionally by the system. Then, eventually, some of these people begin to act out violently and commit some of the very "hate crimes" that this very PC system was designed to prevent.

Anyone can relate to the intensity of emotions like anger, frustration, and rage. We have all been there when something makes us so upset that we can't even contain ourselves. This is the authentic nature of our negative emotions and negative emotions create more negative emotions.

Anger is a surface expression that is driven by deeper, hidden emotions that are weaker and desperate like fear, shame, and insecurity. After living with these weaker emotions for a while, they fester and create more of itself then hatred, anger and rage are projected and forced to the surface once the weaker emotions are triggered.

What I refer to as "weak" emotions are not actually weak, they can probably be understood that way but make no mistakes, these emotions are extremely intense and painful. They have to be to create aggressive forces like anger and rage.

The process works almost like a kettle. You are the water, the fire is like the emotions that stays inside you and burn and build up until you start to boil and then suddenly a big blow, which represents anger and rage.

Emotions that are suppressed, festers and grows and the more it's ignored the more it's suppressed and the more it festers and grows until like the kettle they explode. This is what's happening sometimes when we hear of hate crimes in today's world, where political correctness is so heavily pushed and is expected of everyone.

Not everyone's emotional system can keep up with being calm and "chill" as the social justice movements expects them to. Some people are better at composing themselves than others, and there are so many different types of individuals in the world and even in the same interest groups, each individual is living with different emotional systems.

Every person has a different upbringing, mindset and life experiences that cause him or her to be more or less volatile. In the same organized interest group, some people will be more willing to commit anus acts than others. For example, within the Ku Klux Klan, some may be more "sociopathic" than others, some may be more impulsive than others and some are angrier than the rest.

I'm stating this to make the point that, even though you may think the laws and the political correctness policies have everyone in order, there is no way to prevent some people from committing violent crimes if they are the type that is ruthless enough to do it. We cannot stay in our homes and prevent crimes on the outside. As a society, we have to become wiser about our social politics.

What's your P.C. Intention?

You may hear people in our society complaining about political correctness. While their views on the subject are all valid, the intentions are not always positive.

Some people want political correctness to go away because they believe it is getting in the way of expressing themselves. Some people genuinely can see, that in order to resolve our differences, we have to be open and raw, so we can look at the deepest truth for what it is and represents.

Then there are those who want to have political correctness gone so they can get to say and do things to hurt others.

I see political correctness as a block that stands between the people and their emotional, spiritual healing. We must be truthful to ourselves about everything we think, believe, and feel in order for us to understand our minds and what drives our negative beliefs about others.

Unbiased or PC?

Another important thing to understand about humans and emotions is that most things we do and say are related to our personal feelings. It is not easy to separate a situation from how we feel about it personally. In other words, we aren't really indifferent or objective about most things. Most of the times a person's feelings are based on how something is affecting them on a subjective level. In my opinion, this is why a justice system can never be 100% "just," fair, or effective.

Judges, lawyers, police officers (let's call them law workers) are all "personalizing" (taking it personally) their legal cases, 99% of the time. They may try to make unbiased, objective decisions for their legal cases but whether or not those decisions were objectively fair or made logical sense, that Judge, or officer still had their own personal feelings wrapped up in the case. They just didn't act on them.

People who work within the law enforcement/justice system (law workers) are not Robots, they are human beings first, and a Human is a highly emotional and sensitive being.

Whenever something occurs between other people, the law-worker will "personalize" it in different ways.

One way is if a person involved has something in common with the law worker, (or something he identifies with/as) like race, gender, color, religion. The law worker will see himself in that person's position and he will take their situation personal. The details of the situation may logically make sense for the other party to win but emotionally the law worker wants the person who has something in common with him to win.

Another way in which a human being will personalize a situation between other people is actually in an opposite kind of case, where for example, if you are a police officer and there is an occurrence in which the people involved have nothing in common with you (people you don't identify with). You will "personalize" this in a different way. In this case, the decisions you make can come from the prejudice that you usually feel towards one or both of the parties involved.

In the first scenario that I described, the law worker's personal feelings were in line with identity favor and in this case, the police officer's personal feelings are related to "dis-identity" prejudice. We are still dealing with "personal feelings" in both situations.

In this situation, the officer, may make unfair decisions based on his own abilities to rule from his personal feelings or what made sense to him logically. But he cannot avoid having his personal prejudice or biased feelings involved whether he had ruled from them or not.

Personalized feelings become bias because of how you identify yourself with, and or what your perceptions are of the people involved and how they affect your life.

Maybe some people reading this passage will disagree that most of the times, the people in working in the justice system have biased feelings when trying the cases. The reason this is hard to believe is because the public has seen different cases where the law worker or officer had in fact rule in favor of the people he has zero in common with. This happens because some law workers choose to rule from "their heads" and not their emotions or personalized feelings.

"Ruling from your head" deals with the logic, practicality, and rationality of the details in a particular case and or just how obviously guilty or not guilty someone is. "Ruling from emotions" is making judgments and decisions from your personal or personalized feelings.

Whether the ruling is being made from the head or emotions, the bias or prejudice feelings still exist, they just chose to not act on them.

A law worker may choose to rule from the head for a few reasons. One reason is, out of fear of getting in trouble with the public and or the strict politically correct justice system itself. Another reason is to avoid dealing with his own conscience.

There are levels of compassion or empathy, a law worker may feel towards people they have nothing in common with, but most of the times, the level of bias or prejudice will surpass the level of compassion and the mind can still choose to rule from either one.

For some people ruling from their heads as oppose to their emotions, can become easy, especially for those people who work in the law enforcement/justice system, because they have been doing it for a long time.

The fact that they have the option of making decisions from our heads or personal feelings, means that there are cases where a judge, jury, officer do in fact operate from their partial feelings.

Over the past few decades in America since political correctness had become expected from people especially from the "authorities." It became hard to tell if a law worker is being biased or not because the system had changed, and racism was not as open as it was in the 60's and back. This means that there may have been unfair verdicts and decisions that weren't questioned because the public would like to believe that all of a sudden, human beings became 100% un-prejudice, unbiased and objective with their feelings.

Whenever the justice system was challenged, it had always triggered a social, political pandemonium that would result in conflicts and even riots. It would create this platform where the intentions of the justice/law worker and the system are questioned, and their authenticity is debated.

One such case was the Rodney King beating trial from 1991 to 1992 in Los Angeles. This case led to the unfair acquittal and verdict of White police officers who committed a violent "crime" against Mr. Rodney King.

I believe that when these things happen people become even more afraid to question the Justice system, from a fear that it will lead to a large public uproar. This also causes a quiet, subconscious notion to be interpreted by the population. This notion says, "if people and the justice system, feel this strongly to prove that they are not prejudiced, racist, or biased, then maybe they are not." It then becomes even harder for people to see and understand the truth about the Justice System and law enforcement.

It is hardly possible for anyone to not have biases in today's world. Maybe in a number of future generations, when we learn to value the truth of our emotions but for now we all have it inside of us to be this way.

The collective consciousness of Humans today is highly ego driven. We all separate ourselves with identity. When we see something happening to someone, we have something in common with us. Identity (ego) causes us to feel like it's happening to us and so the situation is "personalized", this way. Then something interesting occurs.

The ego has two main objectives, to be right and to be good. We feel like it's happening to us so now we must prove how the person we identify with is right and is good. In other words, you see people you have things in common with as "yourself," so now you must defend "yourself."

This is why its next to impossible for anyone (law worker or civilian) in today's world to be totally objective, impartial or unbiased.

~~~~*

After years of practicing political correctness within the courtroom and within law enforcement, people's minds became so trusting that the PC movement has somehow engulfed any shred of bias that the law-workers may have had.

Also, the "officialness" and the formality of the law enforcement, justice system and the Government itself had tricked us. We allow these things to blind us to the fact that the people working in these organizations are living beings with flesh, blood, tears, fears, insecurities and every feeling that there is to be felt. They are just like you and no amount of professional training can separate them from their natural human instincts.

The Deadly Truth About being P.C.

Our actions and personalities will only mirror what's happening inside of us. Whether we are expressing the absolute truth of ourselves or the lie we want people to believe, this is still a reflection of our inner self.

Political Correctness causes people to ignore the mental and emotional truth and express a false layer of themselves.

Every time you are trying to be politically correct, you are lying to avoid conflict and or to get approval. This is understandable as people in general wants to be seen as good.

When dealing with the subject of racism, white people try the hardest to be politically correct because they have more resistance to the topic of race than any other group.

White people were known throughout history to be the most aggressive when it comes to the oppression of people of color. The white people of today are deeply ashamed of their past. Most Caucasians live in a world of absolute guilt and shame when it comes to racism. So not only are most whites willingly politically correct but also it is highly expected of them.

They try hard to not offend because they are extremely afraid they will be perceived as being the same people as their "evil" ancestors. They also are not sure what their feelings are towards certain races, so being extra careful and polite is an attempt to convince themselves of just how tolerant and accepting they are and to mentally eradicate any potential prejudice that may exist. Also, to prove to the world that they are not trying to repeat history.

Racial "minority" groups like black Americans who believe they are/were at the receiving end of white people's racism, demands political correctness from white people. This is their way of trying to protect their feelings from being hurt.

When people's feelings get hurt, it triggers feelings of powerlessness. Most black people are ashamed of powerlessness, so they may choose to not show the obvious actions, evidence, and symptoms of it. The powerlessness that is triggered by hurt feelings is then replaced by a certain pride, aggression, and even arrogance that demands white people to be politically correct.

This is done as an unconscious attempt to disguise powerlessness as pride that will be interpreted as power and strength. Along with this is the fact that non-whites and "minorities" in general are not expected to be as PC when expressing their feelings. Black people are allowed to say just about anything about whites without hardly any social or legal consequences. Black people, for a very long time, would say anything to and about white people. Blacks do this while expecting white people to understand, agree, and be ok with it all.

Maybe for a while, white people accepted this as reality because of their own guilt and shame but at some point, people in the white community will start to see this as unfair and a double standard.

This is something that seems to naturally happen in any situation where one group is/were oppressed by the opposing "privileged" group. Example, men, and women, Rich and poor, fat and skinny, attractive and ugly; the side that is known to be "disadvantaged" were always allowed to be open and honest about their feeling towards the other side. Sometimes these feelings can be taken to extreme levels where the other side is triggered and hurt but are not expected or allowed to react.

There are times when black people would say things that would upset white people and whites would not react because of fear of being labeled a racist. While this is socially accepted, it is and always has been creating major underlying problems for society.

Here is why:

In this book, I've mentioned a few times that all human beings are racist to some degree, White people, of course, are no exception. When whites watch black people talk about them, saying all kinds of disparaging things, while can't do the same or respond expressing what bothers them. It creates a build-up of anger, mixed with existing racist feelings. Whites may not be a "disadvantaged" group per se, but they still have feelings and are hurt like everyone else.

People's feelings and emotions are more impactful and powerful and have a stronger influence on their actions than their thinking, logical mind. This all means it's not possible for white people to be "triggered" and pushed by other people's opinions about them without having cases of violent racist outbursts from members of their community at some point.

The perceived double standard of this one-sided political correctness will also cause white people to develop an interest in using the media to force non-whites in becoming Politically correct towards them and now political correctness has hit an "all-time impossible high", where no one from any community can speak their truth.

The more this policy is accepted, the stronger it gets, and the dangerous underlying counter-productive effects of political correctness will persist and possibly spiral into extremely unfortunate occurrences and events. This is almost an inevitable state because of the action-reaction "principle." This is a natural flow of opposing energies.

Black people's requirement of white political correctness is an unconscious quest for power. White people will subconsciously notice this certain tactic of black people and react by pleading for political correctness while subconsciously/unconsciously trying to take back their power.

Most white people are in denial about the power they do have. They are also extremely afraid losing this power, this is not because they are born evil but because the human mind in general works this way and any race of people in their position would be the same.

~~~~*

I spoke in an earlier chapter that, "The look of Power" is a potent concept that keeps racism going. The way the human mind and emotional system operates, it makes each individual desire consciously or subconsciously for the race, they belong to be the most powerful. The ego wants for the people who look like it to have all the power, especially if it has always been that way.

Now, when White people watch black people make demands of them through the government and the media, it creates a belief that the authorities are more on the side of black people, which feels like black people are gaining more favor and therefore more power. In other words, it causes white people to feel as though they are losing their voice and thus their collective power.

When white people start to feel as though, "The look of Power" is no longer White and the people who were the opposite of "The look of Power" is now assuming the power position, when white people start to feel like they no longer have the power that they may feel entitled to, it causes a silent anger in the white community and their racist feelings towards blacks are heightened.

If any person should feel like they are losing their power, they will have strong desires and urges to do just about anything to take it back.

Power and taking back power can mean different things to different people. Maybe for some whites, this means seeing and putting people who look like them in political power and high positions of authority, this could mean making political statements and appeals to get things back the way it uses to be (i.e. "making America great again"). For some Whites, taking back their power means anger, aggression, degradation, violence and even WAR.

~~~~*

CHAPTER 5

How to create a Race War

I believe racial tensions in America and possibly the entire world had never ceased to exist. Even after the 50's, 60's and 70's. But anywhere from early 2012 to present, tensions have been particularly strong, due to high rates of race-related crimes and hate crimes between civilians of different races and also between the police and Black individuals. These unfortunate events resulted in more than just tensions. There were isolated conflicts, cyber feuding, bullying, and some riots.

Most people viewed this new wave of the race problems in America to be a phenomena that came about from "nowhere." This perception stems from a widely believed idea that racism did not exist anymore.

I grew up in the Caribbean and I remember watching movies and maybe documentaries on racism, especially in the month of February. These programs would send both direct and indirect messages that said, "racism was outdated, and it no longer existed anywhere".

Even as a child I would feel some level of concern about these political issues, but I would find myself temporarily laying my worries to rest in the safe place I created from believing that racism is long gone.

The media for one was a major culprit in this "racism is gone" myth.

The media is like a "go to" source for conduct. The media is a platform in which many people look up to and trust, so of course, people believed this lie .

We may speculate now, that there is a deliberate strategy and a conspiracy by the media officials to mislead the public, while continuing to practice white supremacy in hidden and high places.

Maybe this theory has some validity to it but I'm sure some, if not most of the people in the media would fall under the category of the "every day" people who were also convinced that racism is gone.

Whether a conspiracy or not, the media has done a very "good" job of keeping the population fixated on this kind of falsehood.

How "gone" was racism?

The human consciousness has the dual aspects of good and bad or light and dark or positive and negative. People are desperately afraid of their dark side and therefore obsessively want to be good. So, they will hold on to the beliefs like "racism is gone" so as to avoid any run in with their bad, dark, negative (racist) side that will be labeled as evil.

White people held on to the belief that racism was gone because they desperately needed to know that they have changed. Black people held on to it as a safety mechanism.

This is for Blacks to continue to believe that they are safe in the country and in their environments.

In this book, I speak of how the conscious mind practice a belief until it becomes true. It becomes true because people will mostly demonstrate, and practice actions related to what the conscious mind believes or wants to believe, so even the people who are aware that they believe more than just what's in the conscious mind, are too afraid of not being accepted that they too become really good at concealing their negative, racist beliefs. So, in this case, people become even more convinced that racism is no more.

This was interesting for me to watch, as someone who has been keenly observing and studying the human mind, body, body languages and expressions since childhood. I know how to intuitively detect people's true beliefs and sometimes their intentions by just watching their body languages, expressions and even by just how their faces are formed. Your face will always shape into your most dominant mental, emotional state.

Ever since I've been in the USA, I've been observing people and I would wonder why everyone thought racism was gone. Because everywhere I went, in my dark/brown skin, I would watch people's energies and expressions change in my presence. Even when a person is a truly good pretender with the biggest smile and happy demeanor, I could see the truth under the surface expression.

I was also observing the obvious things that most other people were seeing and living while in denial about. Like walking in a mostly all white restaurant or store and see people turn their heads to stare at you. Some would even point at you. The look they give is one that says, "What is she doing in here"? "Or what are they doing in here"?

What about the fact that people weren't shy to express that their parents would be upset if they dated outside their race. Even the fact that most people tend to only hang out with other people from their ethnic or cultural backgrounds.

There are many Black people (me included) that will tell you that some white people cannot make eye contact with us. However, (at one point in time) some of these very black people would ask if racism still exists, or say it didn't exist anymore. (This avoiding eye contact would happen with about 90% of white people that I encounter).

You may say, "Well these situations aren't actually demonstrating racism." You would say this to me if you are one of the majority of humans who do not quite understand how the racist mind really works, the different levels of racism and the different forms it can take.

Think about this, if you truly feel that someone is your "equal," would you have a problem with them dating your daughter or son? If you truly saw someone as good enough, their color, race or religion would not cause you to dismiss them.

If you were ok with sharing space with someone of another race, you would not need to turn, stare, or point at him or her if they walked into a restaurant, store, church, school etc.

Racism manifests itself in these subtle forms, because we live in a society in which the government has strict laws against overt discrimination and racial abuse. Most people will not express blatant racism if they know that they will get in serious trouble.

If there weren't social and legal policing of hate crimes and racial discrimination, there would still be large numbers of people exercising the Jim Crowe's policies and beliefs. Because let's face it segregation didn't actually go away, it was always still here. Legally it was taken away but socially people were and are still very segregated.

This further shows and proves that the eradication of racism will not solely depend on some governmental or legal act. Its people, it's you, it's me, it's us.

~~~~*

The beginning of the ending of our denial phase started around early 2012. I migrated to America from Jamaica in the early 2000's. Therefore, I spent almost 10 years observing this passive racism and the denial and obliviousness of it all. I had become confused at one point, wondering, "well what exactly is racism? I thought, "if the only type of racism is the active, violent, "Jim Crowe-ing", Cross burning, body lynching, "nigger calling" type, then in that case, racism is gone after all".

Racism was "so gone," yet now in 2015 going on to 2016, we are looking at what may be a build-up to a possible war, between Black Americans and White Americans.

So how did we move from a perceived post-racial America to a potentially pre-race war society?

After the period of the 60's unto the 70's and 80's when political correctness started to seep into the collective mindset, the racial tension began silently. People would either put on a false exterior and or continue to segregate while being cordial. Everything had to be PC and parents started to teach their children to be tolerant of "those who were different."

Life in America took a different political turn. A turn that happened because of a choice. A collective choice to "do the right thing".

People forgot that just before that "right" choice was made collectively; the same human collective were expressing and spewing racist hatred and bigotry. So, what happened to that bigoted mindset? Did it just suddenly jumped right from people's bodies as the decision was made to do and say the right thing? What happened to the previous generation of people who were openly bigoted?

The older ones who came from the era of open and honest bigotry. Did they just drop dead?

People don't understand that a choice is just that, a choice. If I'm running, I could make a choice to stop running but it doesn't mean that my thoughts and feelings about running are all gone. I can sit, and then choose to stand; this doesn't mean that I don't have thoughts about sitting down. I could say bad words or choose not to, this does not mean I won't think those bad words.

If I know I could get in deep trouble for saying these bad words and taking bad actions, then I will make a choice to not say those words or take those actions. However, the original thoughts, emotions, and feelings that lead to those bad words and actions will still exist inside of me. Doing the "right thing" is not always doing the "true thing."

The population of white people that existed in and around the time when Political correctness became "the thing", were direct descendants of some of those who lived in and supported the policies of Jim Crowe-ism. The Jim Crowe generation had children, then their children, had their own children.

Some of the white people in these later generations, held on to and practiced the "old" racist way of thinking. They openly demonstrated racist behaviors, and directly taught their children to be overt racists.

The White people who genuinely wanted to do what's right would out-rightly teach their children to be tolerant. While in one of these cases the people had good intentions, both cases are detrimental and are ultimately doing the same thing.

Here is why:

When a parent tells a child to be tolerant or accepting of others, that parent is indirectly telling that child that there is something wrong with "those people". If that parent didn't see something wrong with "those people," there would not be a need to be tolerant or not tolerant. Whenever you have to tolerate or accept someone, it's an indication that you find them intolerant and unacceptable.

Teaching tolerance and acceptance to children (or adults) will only work in reverse. The mind will notice the indirect underlying truth and it subconsciously interprets the message for what it is. And whatever the truth is, is what you will show in your actions, without you even knowing it.

So, the actions that were taken to fix the damage were actually adding to it.

Most of the people who indulged in the teaching of tolerance and acceptance truly wanted to be "good," they just didn't know how. They still had racist feelings but didn't know what to do with them. The difference between these people and the people who are overt racists, are their intentions. They were/are both racist, but their intentions were different.

This idea of tolerance and acceptance training is the process of how racism lived on into today's world because people thought that teaching and practicing tolerance is what would change the world, but it only served as a "surface" attempt to use conscious lies and actions to cover a subconscious truth.

Not only did teaching "tolerance and acceptance" didn't work, it actually taught us to hate even more.

The tolerance campaign wasn't all bad because just like it had good intentions, it along with integration did one good thing. It created grounds for black people to be seen as "normal" citizens of society, on some level.

After a while, it became a norm for black people to be free human beings instead of slaves or isolated by segregation. This was somewhat of a good first step in introducing integration. The later generations of non-blacks have become accustomed to seeing black people from all social status, rather than growing up in a society where it is normal to see other human beings, being degraded to the "level" of a Crow.

Tolerance teaching and integration helped to normalize what wasn't normal at one time.

While this was, or seemed like a fair start, it was only 10% effective and was not enough.

~~~~*

In a world where we know so very little of what works (on a psychological level) to create peace, allowing political correctness and "tolerance training", to lead the way was like treating an open wound with unknown chemicals and hoping it will heal over time. This idea, as we can see now, was a slippery slope. People were just left to try to get along while having unresolved issues and the denial of these issues.

The people who had their original overt white supremacist agenda still had their "evil" needs and intentions. They needed to be on top while keeping black people at the bottom.

There were those white people who felt this very way to a smaller degree but aren't necessarily aware of it. These are the people who genuinely wanted to become "tolerant and accepting" of black people. They too had and still have a subconscious desire to be above black people, but most of them don't know this about themselves because they are living a state of split consciousness.

There is a part of them that truly wants to do "good" but there is also the dark side of their being (and all people) that is inherently racist. Within this dark side of the human consciousness is the need to know that "I am above someone."

This emotional state is without a doubt, an unavoidable one, as it is being facilitated by what is known as the human ego. The human ego will always believe it is better and bigger than someone or something else. (The ego has to be this way).

So both the liberal whites and the right wingers, have an egotistical need to be above black people, it's just that the need is stronger in the "rightist." and some of the "rightists" are much more aware of it, whereas the leftists are less aware of it and they may have more of a conscience and their intentions may be less sinister than the intentions of overt racists.

"Building War Momentum"

When the Political Correctness and tolerance campaign began, things started to change politically and socially but psychologically and emotionally people still had a racist mentality and some of these people still had a sinister agenda that was existing underground.

There were so many "post-racism" and "post slavery" problems that were hanging over in this supposed new "no racism" society. White people's issues of entitlement weren't resolved and black people's long living mental trauma was still alive and active.

Black people were (and still is) suffering from the negative after-effects of slave programming. This is a generational problem that causes a people to lack the emotional, mental strength and resources it takes to progress socially and economically.

Now we have a population of people, being left to get along with each other while having the very psychological problems that initially created the problem of racism.

Black people's collective race-related trauma is one that extends to, a perceived inability to create security and stability for their community.

This would spark a social and governmental interest in creating ways to aid the black community to achieve against the odds since "the dice are loaded." This gave birth to organizations whose objectives were to ensure some level of "equality" within the educational and employment sectors. One such organization is Affirmative Action.

Educational and labor institutions had to secure and reserve spaces for people who were likely to experience discrimination. When these programs began it was probably needed because, coming directly out of an era of open and systematic racism, people needed to know that there was some level of fairness and equality being introduced to the school and workforce and "minorities" had an equal "shot" at education and occupation.

In my opinion, Affirmative Action should have been a temporary trial operation that is put in place with the intention to eventually find a more effective, permanent alternative. While it was necessary, it has caused, and is still causing extra problems for black people.

~~~~*

The double standard of one-sided Political Correctness and one-sided race pride became the norm in American society. White people were expected to walk on chalk line to accommodate black people. White people were made to never express White pride while black people could be allowed to express their black pride. This was the route taken, not because it was the best, but because it was the best one known.

For some white people, these policies were seen as special treatment for black people and minorities and an unfair double standard, which felt like discrimination towards them.

The "nice" liberal leftist whites went along with it because they believed (or wanted to believe) that they were ok with it. Other Whites may have been vocal about the way they felt about these systems, but this was not aired in the media very much.

For a while, the nation may have assumed that most White people were fine with this "special treatment" of black people because the backlash was not getting a lot of media attention.

This is where things got extremely problematic. Remember I just said that the deeper psychological problems for both white people and black people were not solved?

If these psychological issues were never resolved, the original forces that were driving overt racism were still there but were being suppressed because of this new "do the right thing" movement.

What do we know now about suppressed beliefs and feelings? They will remain suppressed, stay there, grow, and fester unless they are thoroughly addressed by going into the subconscious mind.

Leaving these unresolved issues to fester was bad enough on its own but now blacks were given special treatment and the freedom to express one-sided race pride.

The reality of whites having all the power and privilege resulted in them having an unconscious automatic expectation and entitlement for this power. This only means that the people who didn't have the power will pose a threat to the "powerful ones." Not only that, the people in power (whites) depends on the "powerless" to keep them feeling powerful. (One side has to be down for the other to be up).

Any person (white or not) who've always had "power" will see the special treatment of others as a loss of power and privilege for him.

I don't expect you as a white person to agree. (Do remember these mental states are mostly subconscious).

No one ever wants to lose power. The need, love, and desire for power is an extremely intense one. It is by far the most desperate emotional need. Power for the emotional system is what food is to the physical body. If it can't get it, the consequences will be dire.

Your physical body will die without food, but your emotional system won't die without power, instead, it does one of two things or both. Without power, your negative emotions stay inside of you and build up and or blow up in a violent rage.

This is the order of how this mental process flows:

White people have been in power for a very long time - They love and need this powerful position - in order for whites to remain in this "power" position, black people had to be powerless. Black people's position of lack of power lead to requirement for special treatment and one-sided political correctness - White people saw this as more privilege and power for blacks and therefore a loss of power for them.

Whites started to feel extremely powerless because the people who use to be at the bottom were getting some of the privilege that they felt entitled to - White people were frustrated and angry about this which adds to more racist feelings, but these feelings were being suppressed. The suppressed feelings remained subconscious and as a result, festered and grew over time - the more the years pass the stronger the racist feelings and anger became and the more it surfaces itself in different forms. This leads to black people demanding more political correctness which causes white people to feel like they are losing even more power, creating even more racist anger, which comes out even more - black people call for more "PC-ness" and special treatment, which causes white people to suppress their racist feelings even more, which causes more subconscious festering. And therefore, more silent anger and this process continues just like this in a never-ending cycle until it reaches a boiling point where racism is blatant, overt and in our faces again.

Isn't this what we are dealing with today? Isn't this what we have been experiencing since around early 2012?

The sudden wave of "new" racist violence and tension that you see today is like two friends who have been in a quiet feud due to something like deception or disloyalty. No one ever confronts the other, so they never addressed it, but instead kept a fake, inauthentic relationship because they were trying to be nice. The tension got stronger and more intense with time and became more uncomfortable until one day, someone's true feelings jumps out which leads to a big ugly brawl.

Racism is what and where it is today because for years and years we have been overlooking the deeper suppressed level of the human psyche where racist beliefs and feelings grow.

This never-ending cycle has a potential, and today as I write this book, it has an even stronger probability to grow more and more into an all-out RACE WAR.

~~~~*

Humanity has not yet taken a deeper look at the underlying issues to see that, it is not racial profiling, police brutality, racial violence and systematic discrimination in and of themselves that is actually triggering activities that could lead up to a race war. It is actually the anger from the seemingly less dangerous things like one-sided political correctness, special treatment from organizations like Affirmative Action and the perceived double standard of one-sided race and culture (black) pride.

These are the things that create the type of tension and anger that triggers the racial violence that builds up to the bigger war.

This is not to say that white people are "right" if they start a race war. I am actually trying to get the public to understand that we as a nation and a society have to become super conscious of how the policies we put in place to help, is not helping but instead giving us more of what we are trying to avoid. These policies and organizations will eventually create more problems for all of us. And whether we believe people's actions and beliefs are wrong, they are real and are valid.

As a society, we must become more considerate of all people's sensibilities regardless of how wrong we may think they are.

We should introduce possible solutions that will serve all people equally and that is equally fair for all.

More on Affirmative action

As far as I'm concerned, affirmative action enables to disable. It tells minorities that they cannot "do" for themselves. This causes people to remain stuck, depending on Affirmative action. They won't be inspired or motivated to help themselves if they know someone else will do it for them. It also sends a message to the minority communities that they are victims, which causes them to hold themselves back out of fear of not "making it".

Affirmative action is also a problem for the larger society because they see it as a problem. A lot of white people hate the idea of affirmative action, because it seems like special treatment for minorities, but Affirmative action came about due to the "un-special" treatment of blacks.

White people believe it should go away now since we are way past the post-civil-rights era. We are not living in that time, but we have not healed from the pathology that caused the "un-special" treatment of black people.

The Anti-racism laws and guidelines that were enforced by civic organizations only affected systematic discrimination and racism in educational and labor-centered institutions on a legal level. As a result, people chose to discriminate less. However, this could not and did not guarantee that discrimination against blacks would end one hundred percent.

Just because it's illegal to discriminate, doesn't mean that people won't discriminate and even if people say they don't discriminate, this doesn't mean that they won't discriminate. Moreover, it doesn't mean they are not racist.

Laws and strict guidelines that are implemented by civil rights organizations did not and cannot heal people from their racist feelings that causes them to discriminate. So, taking away Affirmative Action will only lead to a re-emerging of discrimination in institutions (on some level).

What we need to do is work on finding ways to heal the nation from whatever is causing racial discrimination. This way, we don't have to worry about as many "un-special" treatments or special treatments for that matter. This is when we can "do away with" organizations like Affirmative Action.

<u>Change? Or more of the same?</u>

We came this far, still dealing with the same problems and now watching the build-up of overt racism. With this process, you would think that more people would see that it is a cycle and a vicious one that will continue if we don't try something different.

This political system is not trying to do something different, they are trying to enforce more of the same.

People on both political parties are ultimately asking for the same life that we had before this new up wheeling of overt racism. The "leftists" are calling for more Political correctness and the "Rightists" (some of them) are constantly trying to deny the legitimacy (and sometimes the existence) of racism.

Both sides are unknowingly doing the same thing. What they are both doing is using these strategies and claims to avoid dealing with the real issue, which is racism.

They are doing this to avoid the pain, shame, and the discomfort that comes with the truth that they are both racist.

Enforcing more Political Correctness, will push the truth out of the way, suppressing it to avoid the discomfort. Denying racism is another form of suppression that tells the mind that it does not have to deal with the truth because the "truth" does not exist.

So now we see that the Right and the Left aren't that different. They want the same things.

CHAPTER 6

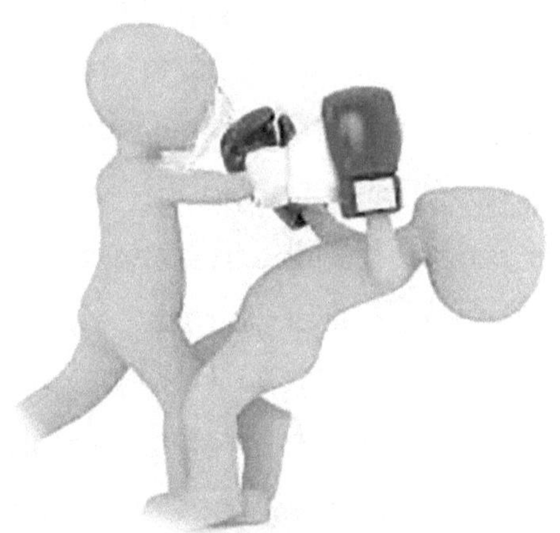

How to really create a Race war

Now that I've explained, the deeper things that could lead up to a race war between black people and white people in America, I hope and believe you understand and it resonates.

But I'm going to tell you that it doesn't stop there because it didn't begin there. I am about to show you that there is a more hidden aspect that has remained hidden because it is easily overlooked. It is easily overlooked, not only because it is super subconscious but also because it gets thrown into the category of small, insignificant and unimportant.

I just spoke of how we spend our time and energy focusing on the bigger things that we believe could cause a race war, like hate, white on black attacks, police shootings, antagonism. We focus on these things, so much, that we miss that most of the anger that builds up into war-like violence stems from things like, special treatment, one-sided race pride and political correctness etc.

However, I have found that these issues are still quite "surfacey".

What I am going to tell you is that there is a deeper level or layer of our subconscious mind that, when triggered creates an even stronger emotional force that creates a warmonger mentality.

In chapter three, I spoke of "The look of power". I explained that, so much of what created racism is based in the seemingly small concepts of looks and beauty, and most people don't catch on to this because it's perceived as a small unrelated issue.

Just like that piece, when it comes to war, we totally miss the meat of it because of focusing on issues that we believe are more important.

As I said in that chapter, the two main ingredients for racism and racial strife is 1. The look of Power and 2. Competition. The competition aspect of it is one main thing that feeds into the potential of a race war.

If you didn't know, I'll tell you now that wars are actually competitions. People create wars because they want to win these wars. The war is usually a huge monumental event that results in calamity and adversity. It's so big that we don't see that it's a competition and that the competition started long before the official war event. And the competition started with very "small", hidden, seemingly unrelated things.

Most minds don't register it this way because the war is played out by the war mongers themselves who also don't understand how deep the competitive aspect of it all runs and so they present it as something bigger.

For example, a race war between Black people and White people would be the surface competition that hides the "smaller" things that they are actually competing with.

<u>Let's discover what are these "smaller" competitions that creates the bigger (war) competition.</u>

I've found that the things we compete with are the "little" things in our lives that we are most sensitive about. These are usually the things we identify with and as. Meaning, its, everything about ourselves that makes us who we are. Our identity will, most of the times, be the things about ourselves that we can't change like gender, color and race.

Being that you can't change these things about yourself, you will want them to be the best because you cannot escape them. You will want every aspect of your identity to win.

- If you are a female, you want females to win over males.

- If you are a man, you want men to win over women.

- If you are white, you want white people to win.

- If you are Black, you want black people to win.

- If you are a white female, you will want white females to win.

- If you are a black man, you will want black men to win.

- If you are American, you want Americans to win.

- If you are an American white male, you want white American males to win. And of course, this goes on and on and it can be very general or very specific identities.

Your ego wants all your identity aspects to be the best so whenever it feels threatened or challenged, it becomes not just afraid but desperately afraid. A very sensitive part of the self is triggered. This is also the part, where we are hurt the most, mainly because of the "knowing" that, you can't change this part of yourself. This is the "hurt feeling" level of the self.

The ego recognizes this hurt and sensitivity as weaknesses. The ego now seeks to disguise this "weakness" as strength. It covers and disguises the perceived weakness with aggression, anger, antagonism, and bravado. In simpler terms, this is how the warmonger mentality is created.

What I'm ultimately saying here is, what has never been said. That what we know to be the colossal size, untouchable, governmental, intimidating event of war is always been driven by the "little" things that hurt our "little feelings."

Going back to the topic of race war; what I've observed is that, the build-up of anger from years of mental/emotional suppression and censorship of white people's negative feelings towards black people's special treatment, one-sided political correctness, the blaming and shaming of white people and the one-side (black) race pride etc. were also packed with growing hurt feelings.

<u>These hurt feelings are related to things like:</u>
- The belief that black people are genetically inferior.
- The belief that blacks are less intelligent.

- Non-blacks saying that no one should or wants to procreate with blacks.
- The idea that Blacks/Africans are less than human.
- The popular opinion that the Black/African features are less than attractive.

On the other side:

- Black people expressing that white people's genes are recessive.
- The belief and showcasing of black biological advantages and potency.
- The expressed belief of black male sexual advantages.
- The belief that Black men have bigger penises.
- Interracial relationships between white women and black men.
- White women professing their adoration for black men.
- Black people telling white people that they age terribly.

And so much more.

So how do we move from these "small" things to war?

When you separate yourself in groups based on racial or cultural identity, you will automatically see the other group as your opponent, which means you will be comparing yourself to them on every level and with every aspect of identity. If you believe that you can't quite measure up to the other group in certain areas, you'll create a bigger competition like a fight or a war to do two main things. 1. Disguise and mask the "smaller," sensitive stuff. 2. To compensate for the smaller areas you believe you can't/won't win in.

It's like a girl who's lost her boyfriend to another woman, she believes she has lost the competition of keeping the man, so she starts a fight with the other woman to gain back some kind of strength and feel a victory that she lost from losing her man.

<u>In the case of Black people:</u>
- The belief that black people are genetically inferior triggers the warmonger mentality, from black people feeling like they could potentially lose the competition between black genetics and white genetics.
- The belief that blacks are less than intelligent triggers the warmonger mentality from blacks feeling like they have lost the competition between black intellect and white intellect.
- The belief that blacks are less than human triggers black people's war monger mentality from the fear that they have lost the competition of who is more human. Etc.

For White People:

- The fighter mindset is triggered in white people if they believe they have lost the competition between the white penis and the black penis.

- The war mentality is triggered in white people if a part of them feels as though they have to prove who has the stronger genetics.

- The belief that black men are more sexually potent triggers the warmonger mentality within white men as this causes them to feel as if they are losing the competition between white male potency and black male potency.

- Interracial relationships between Black men and White women - White men's warmonger mentality is triggered to fight to take back the power that they've lost in the competition over white women.

- Telling white people things like "they don't matter", "they aren't worth anything", "they should stand down", "they are less important" may cause them to feel insignificant. A war monger mentality is triggered here, because when people feel insignificant, they will do anything to feel the opposite, which may include violence. Think about it, if someone has over-powered you in a fight (war), won't they be (negatively) significant in your life?

These are just some of the examples of how the "smaller" things we compete with will trigger the hurt feelings that build the warmonger mentality. There are so much more that could be added to these lists because the war monger mentality is affected by anything that is meant to be hurtful and anything that makes one feel insecure.

These are the things black people and white people have always been fighting about and what the race war would really represent (on a subconscious level). It is this desperate need to be the best in every area of your racial identity.

The war or fight symbolizes a potential victory in the "little" areas of the self that they are most insecure and sensitive about. These areas of ourselves, we will compare to other people and other groups of people.

This is the concept of "you think you are winning, but I'll show you who is the bigger, "badder," and better man in this game."

The most dangerous aspects of this situation are the areas involving male "power" and male potency since males initiate most wars. Wars are really an expression of the masculine over-compensation. Whenever men feel like they are losing or lacking in one masculine aspect they will use something like fighting and battle to demonstrate and prove their "manly" strengths. This is not just with "race wars." Every war in history was about, the male human species claiming some kind of male potency.

When we hear of nations fighting over land, oil, weapons. What they are really fighting for is their manhood. The land, oil, weapons are just the middle items that stand between their masculinity and the war. These things are what they lay their sense of pride in, to add to their perceived masculine power. These things are also used as a cover to conceal the deeper, "weaker" truth. (May I add that this concealing process is not done consciously or deliberately).

The race war is also a war over sexual male power. The feelings that trigger the war monger energy the most are the ones that involve black male sexuality versus white male sexuality and power.

These days there is a huge collective rival between white men and black men regarding the rise of interracial relationships between white women and black men. This is a very large part of the silent race war that has existed for decades and maybe centuries.

Some people believe that there is the envy of "big black penises" from white men and so there is a fear that black men will be the white woman's object of desire much more than white men.

Whether it is objectively true that black penises are bigger, people (including some white men) believe it's true, so these people will be affected by this belief in a negative way. The tension from this particular issue is quite tight and heavy because it gets even more complex.

For a very long time, white men have either consciously or subconsciously believed that they were superior to black men (and black people). White men have created many theories, belief systems, events, and policies to support this belief. So now that these "inferior" men can actually lay down with white women, it means that the "inferior" men are somehow on the level of white men, which also mean white men are at the level of these "inferior" beings, which means he (white men) is inferior.

This is a huge aspect of white men's subconscious fear of White women being with black men. This mental process will certainly cause White men to develop a desire to destroy black men and subdue them in battle.

There are white men and people who are open white nationalists that present the interracial issue as a threat to white genetic survival. They believe that interracial relationships are wrong because it will be the number one contributor to "a white genocide."

While I believe that many white people in the white community have convinced themselves that this is the reason, they are against interracial love, I don't believe that this is the number one reason. I believe the "white genetic survival" story is mostly used to cover a more fearful reason.

Here's the thing; The world is said to become a brown-skinned world in more than a few decades down the line.

Around that time, most white people, living today will be either dead or extremely old. What is the point of trying preserve "the good white genetics," if you are not going to be here to witness the continuation of it?

Most of the times when a group of people is this irate about anything, it's usually based on something they are in fear of now and not the future.

The problem white men have with black men and white women relationships have very little to do with a possible future white genocide. It has more to do with how it makes them feel now. It makes them feel inadequate now, it makes them feel insecure now, it makes them feel overlooked now, and it makes them feel unimportant now. It makes them feel irrelevant now and it makes them feel inferior now. It's not about the future, it's about now.

White men and black men are in a silent subconscious war for "White Vagina". Since its unconscious, they don't know that the fight is more about their own penis strength and less about the things their conscious minds want to believe, like "white genetic survival."

Even though White Genetic survival is not the biggest part of their fear, it is still a fraction of it. People, in general, want their kind to survive, because it symbolizes their own personal survival. They want the people who they identify with to live forever because in some way it means that they are living forever. It's the ego's need to hold on to the present identity forever, and it's the ego's fear of death.

~~~~*

If my point of view on this whole "race war" matter sounds outlandish or far-fetched to you, I want you to think about something, how many times have we witnessed someone wanting to start a fight because something has hurt their feelings. Most people probably believe that they can distinguish between what triggers the fighting energy within others. Most people seem to think that, what makes us fight are related to the things that frustrate, "pisses of" or aggravates, but the truth is, it's actually the things that hurt.

How many times have we seen men become furious because someone taunts him for being broke or for having a small penis? How many times have we seen a female start a fight because she was told that she is ugly? Or what about a woman who wants to fight another woman because this other woman is prettier?

~~~~*

This new emerging of overt racism is a result of the resurfacing of negative feelings related to frustration and anger but also hurt, and mostly hurt.

Some people base this new racial divide on a myriad of things which includes the belief that "racism is coming back" – "just because."

I say, "racism isn't coming back because racism was never gone". It was still very much here in the (subconscious) mental, emotional level in the form of fear, shame, anxiety, anger, and hurt.

Society sees "weak" emotions as small, petty, irrelevant, frivolous things that will only result in and extends to other small, petty, irrelevant, frivolous things. This makes the potential for a race war even stronger because they will continue to hurt each other with words, assuming it's just little harmless verbal fights.

The verbal jabs create an even stronger competitive force within white people and so they'll want to win. The anger builds up until it spirals beyond our control.

They say, "hurt people, hurt people." The more black people feel hurt by white people's degrading words about them, the more black people say things to hurt white people until it turns from verbal to physical.

For years now, we've carried on a system where it's ok for black people to say and do things to white people that white people cannot say or do to them. This policy came about because of the victim-perpetrator "response principle". Whites were the "perpetrators" in history, so today they have to "walk on chalk line" around the victims. If not, they will be in trouble with not only the media and the public and possibly law.

It gave black people the green light to abuse that "privilege", especially in the later days where there are so many cyber interactions through various internet venues.

This is a danger zone because remember this is where the most hurtful words are exchanged.

Both sides know that a physical fight will not happen through their computer screens, so they just let it all out.

More and more, I see so many cases where black people are just "going for the jugular" and spewing so much hate towards white people, and then white people are doing the same. This kind of conflict is terrible for everyone, but it is especially dangerous for black people.

WHY:

1.   Because this is precisely how to create a race war.

2.   If a race war were to happen it would most likely be initiated by white people - specifically white men. This is not to imply that black men are "soft" or defenseless.

<u>Blacks have to be extra careful because of these following points:</u>

- Black people in America are greatly outnumbered by whites.

Not all white people would support this war and maybe most won't support it, but the number of whites that would support it, is a large enough number to cause considerable damage not only to the black community but also to the country itself.

- The country has a mostly white government.
  You may ask, "what are you saying"? Will the government be involved in a war against black people?
  I say, yes and no. There are those in the government who have good intentions and there are some who don't. There is no way to know "who is whom".

- The government is a mostly white co-operation that is in control of organizations like the military, the police force, the FBI and the CIA. Let's not forget high-level weaponry, scientific/biological warfare and advanced technology. What about the fact that the Government controls the food distributors and water supply.

For these reasons, inciting a race war would not be wise on black people's part. I didn't need to explain all of this, for you to see that black people in America are not prepared or ready for a war.

The biggest problem is that most black people don't even know that they are provoking a war because again "all they're doing is just making fun of white people." "A little name calling and "fun-poking" will ever hurt anyone." "No one is being hurt or harmed here so nothing major will result from it."

Blacks are inciting a race war without knowing they are while lacking the level of defense and resources to measure up to the power structure they are going up against." - "Sounds like a good idea to me."

Now, I may be wrong. There might just a black-owned militant organization somewhere and maybe there is a system operated by black officials who are equipped with very powerful weapons needed to have victory in a war against White America. This is possible but from my point of view, it is more than likely, not the case.

~~~~*

Even if most white people do not support the potential race war, based on what I know about the human psyche, only a small percentage of white people would get actively involved in helping black people in battle.

<u>Here are some reasons why this is:</u>
- There is a fear of, "what other white people are going to think of me," They will see me as "kissing up" to black people, which means they see me as weak."
- The fear that, "my fellow white people are going to think I am trying to be something I am not".

- Some white people believe racism is not their problem, so most would care to an extent but not enough to take part in a massive fight against their own people, where they may die.

- There are white people, radical or not, who are ruthless enough to kill other white people if they are getting in the way of the race war. Once this starts to happen, many White people will get out of the way, because they know their white skin will save them once they are not in the way. Not that they don't care but if most people were, to be honest, they would say that they care more about their own lives than the lives of others.

- The Ego is all about identity, there is an inescapable nature of the ego that has to be right. When you identify as an individual you are identifying as self, so you always have to be right. When you identify with a group, you identify that group as self, so that group has to be right.

For most white people to enter into a war against other whites is for them to say, "we are wrong and not right. This is one of the hardest things for the ego to do.

**~~*~~*

All people can relate to this need to be right. Think about any time in your life, when, maybe you did something wrong; was it easy to admit that you were wrong? It's the same thing when you must apologize to someone. You can't really agree to apologize without acknowledging that you are wrong. This is one main reason why apologies are so hard. Can you relate? Yes, you can.

~~~~*

The belief that some white people have, that racism is not their problem, comes from the reluctance to see how it may really be their problem. This reluctance comes from a fear of evaluating themselves and the fear that if they do, they might find that it is also their problem. Therefore, they reject the issue altogether, to avoid the burden and the work it will take to fix the problem.

The higher social/economic status that whites have over people of color has created this disinterest in "third world problems" including racism. They have confidence that their wealth and sophistication will keep them away from the problems that plague "minorities." They have never truly been in a state where they were the ones being discriminated against at a mass level, so they can't relate. And most don't want to relate.

~~~~*

So much of what I've been explaining here may be interpreted as me, trying to justify white people's lack of interest and possible intentions. It may feel as though I am saying that white people starting a race war would be right. This is not the case.

I think I did a fair delivery on how things could play out on the parts of both white people and black people.

We are dealing with two different people, who live two different lives and therefore two different perspectives. The mind works a specific way but when we are in our own perspective it's hard to understand why others could operate in the selfish way they do.

If we understand that we're using the same mindset but different perspectives, then we could agree that if we were in each other's shoes we would do the same. And from the opposite perspective, the other will seem extremely selfish.

Who is "righter"?

Whatever psychological and emotional state a people are in, they can only be there. They can't be anywhere but there. White people are where they are, and black people are where they are, and guess what? Both white people and black people believe that they are right to be there.

People cannot just choose to be anything but what they are and also what they believe. From white people's perspective, they are right and black people are wrong. From black people's perspective, they are right and white people are wrong.

Black people believe it is right to have one-sided political correctness and one-sided race pride. Some black people believe they are right to say bad things to white people. If white people should initiate a race war, they will believe that they are right to do so.

Everyone has to be right because it's too painful not to. This is one main reason why people in opposition will never see eye to eye. Their positions have to be right.

Let's compare this to nature.

The life experiences of an Alligator will be much different from that of a Goat. They operate, think, and expect different things because their nature and instincts are so different. They are both trying to survive and believe everything they do to survive is right for them to do.

The goat will never understand why the Alligator has to eat him. However, from the alligator's point of view, he's right to eat goats, because he's a carnivore who is hungry.

The goat thinks the Alligator is wrong. The Alligator knows he is right. The Alligator thinks the Goat is wrong for trying to get away. The Goat knows the right thing to do is run away because he loves his life and wants to live.

Do you see this flow? They both live lives that are different and separate, they live lives that are unique to them, valid for them and will only make sense to them. They kind of have the same need (to survive) yet oppose each other.

This is precisely how two opposing perspectives work. They won't agree because from where they are, their individual point of views is both valid and both RIGHT.

They both also have to win. The desperate need to win is an essential state. It is one of the most persuasive, compelling energies in our bodies. Think about anything in your life that you want to win. Even if it's not a competition. It could be an exam or test that you want to pass. (Passing symbolizes winning). Now, can you stop or change this need to win/pass? Go ahead and try to change it. You will soon find that no matter what, you can't.

You have to win, and you have to be right; so, does your opponents. Therefore, if you both have different needs and you are both "right", how could you possibly expect to agree?

Empathy?

There is an aspect of our ego consciousness that exists at some level or another as long as you are in a physical body. The ego thrives on identity and separation. The reason, we are separated is because of identity. Once you've claimed an identity you are separated from others. This is something all physical humans experience.

You identify = separate = disconnect. When you disconnect from something, you won't see it as you. Then you won't feel for it.

For example, if I'm white then you're black, then you are not me, so your problems are not my problems, your interests are not my interests. Your life is not my life, your feelings are not my feelings, your hurt is not my hurt, and therefore we are not one. If you can't see yourself in someone, you may naturally lack empathy, understanding, and compassion for him or her.

The people you separate from, on some level you will see as your opponent and your competition, this causes the lack of empathy to heighten.

This is not because you are evil; it's actually a natural inevitable flow of how our emotional system works.

Humans lack empathy for others mainly because their focus is so invested in their own hurt feelings that it's hard to feel for others especially if we are dealing with feelings that oppose each other.

If we disagree on the same topic, it's hard for me to understand your side because I will be too invested my own feelings about it. Plus, also there is the desperate need to be right. For people with opposing views to express empathy for each other, is for them to indirectly admit that they did or is doing something wrong, which invalidates the very things that they are fighting for. These forces are way too strong for them to access any understanding for each other.

<u>Yet another means to war</u>

There is another issue that I believe is heightening the war monger energy within White people.

This is the asking of whites to take down their confederate flags and the historical artifacts that represent the people and the time in which black people were experiencing the height of overt racist abuse.

Black people's stance on this subject is very valid. It's valid because the images that represent such ugliness in history is and will cause emotional disturbances for them. Even though the black people living today were not living in the time when these symbols were accompanied by open and blatant racial abuse, the thought of what they represent then, can still be traumatic for the mind.

This is one reason why I believe Black people need to work on their fears relative to these images. I also believe white people need to work on the darkness within them that supports the need to display these items regardless of how it may affect others.

I do believe that it's best for Blacks to start their healing process because the way they have been trying to deal with this matter is dangerous.

Black people have been trying to get the government to implement policies for the White nationalists, and the Confederate supporters to put away their flags, signs, and statues.

If you are looking at this matter from your own perspective, you will understand your stance on it to be the right thing because you believe that that flag represents hate and hate are wrong. But from White people's perspective, you are provoking them. You think they are wrong and they think they are right.

When people believe strongly in something, it becomes what they stand for. Even if you think it represents something bad, they still stand for it and people will always fight hard for what they stand for.

The emotional energy of the things they stand for is as equally strong, equally valid, and equally compelling as the feeling you have towards the things you stand for.

Take a minute to reflect on what you as a black person stands for regarding this very issue. Think about how deep your need is to get rid of the Confederate flag and statues, can you stop or even control that need?

Well, the need some white people have to keep their flags and statues is just as strong and firm. They have the same kind of emotions backing up their stance on this subject.

So, when they feel as though the things they stand for are going to be taken away, a war monger energy is triggered within their beings.

<u>Now here are some other factors that need serious consideration as far as this topic goes:</u>

1. When the confederate flags and Confederate statues are removed, what have we really accomplished?

If the Ku Klux Klan, white nationalists, neo Nazi's and others want to kill non-whites, they will do it with or without the flags and the symbols. They don't need these things to kill you if that's what they want to do. So, taking these things away won't actually help in any way.

If anything, it will be one of the biggest catalysts to more racist violence. They already hate you and now you are provoking them by taking away their freedom of expression.

2. Wouldn't you want to know "who's who"?

Wouldn't you want to be able to know who the people that are around you are?

I don't know about anyone else, but I would like to know where and who the white nationalists are by seeing the signs of their territory. For example, if I took a road trip in the South American states, I would feel better when I see certain flags, signs, and symbols so I know how to be cautious and who to trust. When some people have a specific mark, I will know just who I'm around and just where I can be safe.

There is no wrong or right action to be taken as far as the idea of restricting the display of Confederate statues and flags. Both sides want different things and both their stance are valid. This is why a resolution to this issue has to start with the understanding that it has to begin at an emotional level.

Black people have to work on the emotional pain that is triggered by these images and white people has to understand that, most of their motives for displaying these images are based on their own unresolved pain.

People have to work on their weak points and fears regarding these subjects until they are at a point where they can agree on what is the right policy for this matter.

Snatching down Confederate statues and flags in the political climate which we exist in today, will only cause an uproar and a rage that can escalate into mass violence and destruction.

We have to wake up and acknowledge our reality for what it is. Hate exists, Racism exists, wickedness exists, and the symbolism that represents these things also exists.

When black people and social justice warriors try to take away the symbols that represent hate, they are doing this to eradicate hate. But they are only doing this to "make believe." To create the reality, we want to exist instead of acknowledging the truth that is in our faces.

It doesn't take a Rocket Scientists to realize that the hate is not within the symbols and the flag, hate is within the people. I am still lost, as to why all people are not thinking this way.

CHAPTER 7

Are Cops Racist?

In today's world, people use things like social media to spew their honest, raw, and disturbing views on current affairs. Sometimes there are bullying, and antagonism related to race and racism on the internet. This is just one way in which people try to take their power back. Other ways can be more extreme like gun violence, terrorism, police brutality.

Some people would like to believe that the police are built and trained to be people who can operate and act from an unbiased and un-prejudiced state but what most people fail to realize is that the police force and legal officials are just people like everyone else. They will mostly act from emotions.

For years in America, there has been a major rift between the police force and the black community. It just so happens that majority of people in the police force are Caucasians.

Around the year 2012 to present (2016) there have been a series of Police shootings and killings of African Americans, which lead to a conflict between, not just the police and the people but also the people and the people.

Conspiracy theorists would speculate the possibility of these shootings being a planned out, strategic operation by the sinister "powers that be." Others believed that this is just racism coming back slowly.

First, let's look at who are the Police.

The police are men and women who get sworn in the law enforcement organization for the physical protection of the people and civil service. This position gives police officers legal rights to be one of the lower levels of authority within the Government. Though this position is lower, it still lends the officer the power to enforce order and control on a hands-on level, directly with civilians.

Anybody who finds himself or herself in any position of power, had a desire to be there. People who desire to be in the police force, their main objective is Authority. Consciously they believe that they want to protect and serve, but on a deeper level, a big part of their need to be in the police force is stemming from a much darker place.

Most people who end up in positions of authority (let's call them, "the Authority figure") are those who had dealt with situations and people who made them feel extremely powerless at some point in their younger lives. They then spend their lives needing to feel powerful. Needing to take back any power that was taken away from them. The people in their environment that they believe represent disorder, misconduct, and indecency will be at the receiving end of their judgment and subjection.

People who crave authority because of feeling deeply powerless will see the "lawless, indecent, rejects of society" as the target of their subjection because they are constantly looking for someone to feel superior to.

The "indecent rejects" are " easy targets" as society, in general, sees them as inferiors and therefore will be perceived as inferior to those who are here to "protect and serve".

Most people in legal/governmental authority, don't know that their position is a guise. They don't know that it is an unhealthy means for reclamation of power and significance. Someone or something in their childhood was in control over them, now they subconsciously see control as power because of the way it affected them. They don't know how to liberate themselves from their conformities and the fear of being judged, so a criminal, who is the opposite of the conformist mentality is subjected to be controlled by them.

In a way, this is a subconscious envy that people in authority have of the criminal's ability to do things that they believe they can't do (i.e. be rebellious). The rebelliousness represents a kind of power that "the authority figure" believes he can't have. (It could be because this is the kind of power he lost as a child).

A person who is in any position of authority, from a security guard to a governmental official will usually be extremely critical of others. This person will be just as critical of himself. His mind will always search for people and things to be critical of. He does this to shift the negative self-inflicted criticism away from himself unto something else and thus he feels better about himself. A criminal is a perfect example of this "something else."

There are some traits and attributes that are considered undesirable, they can be a character flaw or a natural human quality. For example, being black can be perceived as being in the same social class as the most degenerate, immoral being. Blackness is one of the traits that the racist aspect of the human mind sees as inferior. So black mixed with criminality is seen as the worse combination. People who pride themselves in being upstanding, ethical, citizens, then see black people as second-class members of society. The high crime rate in the black community does not help.

<u>"De-Policing" the Police?</u>

The police officer, who, like all Human beings is racially prejudiced, cannot separate his prejudice feelings from himself just because he's a police officer. He is feeling all the emotions that every human is feeling along with the thoughts that accompanies these emotions.

If you are a police officer, who is regarded as a valued member of society, who grew up in an environment that praises certain types of people (like Police officers) and look down on others (like blacks and criminals), you are also going to look down on these types of people.

If this is the case, then there is a strong potential that some of these emotional human beings called cops are capable of things like the degradation, profiling, abuse and even murder of the people who carry these undesirable characteristics.

Society already has an existing prejudice towards the black community as a whole, and then within the group, are people who, commit crimes in high numbers. Most people outside the black community will not have high regards of black people.

So, what about the police who spends a great amount of time having first-hand experiences in the environments of these "black criminals", interacting with them on a daily basis and having to deal with many of their criminal activities.

It's not easy for any human being to perceive something as bad without responding to it as such.

A police officer reacting negatively towards a black person is not always noticed by that black person. Most people are not trained to read and understand what different body languages and facial expression mean or how to know when someone is not showing their true feelings. Therefore, a racist cop will have all kinds of negative feelings and thoughts about you and you may not see it.

Cops are human beings who carry around negative feelings and like any person, can be triggered, irritated and angered which are the states that lead to violent actions especially if provoked.

Can anyone honestly say that they were angry with someone without judging them based on different aspects of who they are? Can you really say you ever got into an altercation with someone of another race without thinking derogatory thoughts relative to their race? I don't even believe that is possible. In fact, every time we interact with someone, even just passing them on the street, we get thoughts about what that person looks and seem like and what you believe about "people like them."

We are constantly "sizing people up" and judging them based on the differences between you and them. So of course, if you have to deal with people who are "disrupting" society's order, you will be judging them, stereotyping them negatively which is the root of either what results in verbally or physically abusing them.

Take into consideration, the "psychology" of the "authority figure" (police officer) that I explained earlier, mixed with existing feelings of not valuing the life of the "black criminal" or black person.

I believe this "psychology" of the authority figure is the very pathology that drives extremely racist people to join the police force, where they can live out their fantasies of subduing the people they want to continue to see beneath them.

There is a possibility that some police officers and other law enforcement workers, went into the force with sinister intentions that are motivated by their racist beliefs.

-We wouldn't know who they are as people's thoughts and intentions aren't written on their foreheads.

I believe there are some men who get into law enforcement with the intention to take revenge on, and over-power the specific type of people that contribute to or trigger their feelings of powerlessness. This type of people may just be a particular race of people.

For example, if a white man had experiences where he was bullied or made to feel less of a man by a black man; the "force" may be an attractive field for him to find opportunities to take down the men who helped to create this sense of weakness.

It's simply the reclamation of power over another person under the guise of enforcing the law.

Author's Perspective:

I was watching a media program that was recorded in recent years. It featured a Ku Klux Klan member who chose to remain anonymous. He sat in the dark and spoke through a "robotic voice changer" as he proceeds to tell his interviewer that, within the "Klan", are a growing number of men that includes paramedics, Doctors, lawyers, Judges, politicians and Police officers.

Now, when we hear of cases where a police officer was said to had abused his power, it could very well be a situation where a "super" racist officer is using his given authority to carry out own racist agenda.

~~~~*

There is a belief that in order to lessen the apparent racist altercations and occurrences between the police and "minorities," better training is needed for cops.

What most people don't realize is that no amount of training is going to stop a racist ill-intentioned police officer from attacking a black person. When they speak of "proper training", they are speaking of making improvements in the way police officers handle situations on a professional level.

Racist feelings are emotional, and training is practical and professional. Learning more policing skills will not take away one's racist feelings.

Because someone mentally comprehends the guidelines that were set out for him, does not mean that emotionally, he can control his urges to do bad things. When most police officers do bad things to people they are not operating from a place of incompetence, they are operating from a place of emotional darkness. Professional and skilled training does not affect one's emotions in this way.

~~~~*

Let's not disregard the truth that some people in "minority" communities do provoke police officers and again, in these cases, the police officers are humans that can feel harassed, angered and even hurt to the point of fury.

I would like to point out that not all police officers or people within law enforcement have bad intentions. In addition, remember all Cops are humans and all humans are racist/prejudiced at different degrees. Some officers are more racist than others. And not all officers who are highly racist are also interested in committing racial hate crimes. Some officers (and people in general) who are extremely racist may be consumed by their own conscience or for some reason, is able to control their urges to hurt people.

This, you should know

There is one super important thing that we should understand about all humans, from the police to convict. We are all born with all the same emotional foundations. Each emotion is in a potential state to exist at different levels. Meaning all people will have more or less of the same emotional conditions and therefore more or less of the same personality states that are created by those emotions. These emotions grow, fester, and then come out as good or bad actions.

From our most positive doings to the bad and even the most gruesome acts, are all driven by these emotional roots. The people who can go through life being mostly benevolent also have an emotional base from which certain so-called evil intentions grow.

We all have a dark side and a light side. (Some people have a bigger dark side than light side). Within the darkness live all the negative emotions, each at different levels.

What am I saying here?

I am saying that the bad and evil qualities that we see in other people are coming from a root/source that exists in all of us.

Most people aren't aware of this and some are in denial, which is one reason, why we are so quick to judge and condemn other people's actions without understanding the deeper motives behind their actions.

Our emotions are extremely powerful energies. Think about your emotions as living consciousness that is just as real as you are, and just like you, they have their own wants and needs. Understanding this will make it easier to see just how intensely desperate emotions can be.

You are a physical vessel that is transporting different non-physical energies around. Your emotions are these energies. Your emotions want what they want and need what they need and if they don't get it, they will flare up out of control and sometimes explode.

When your emotions flare up, you flare up because they are a part of you, just like your physical body parts.

If your liver is sick then you are sick, if your Intestines are infected, then you will feel pain from it and act like someone who is in pain. It's like a bomb inside a building, when that bomb goes off the whole building goes off with it.

You have the same relationship with your emotions. Your emotions react to your thoughts and you react to your emotions with your expressions, actions, and decisions.

Negative emotions lead to actions that range from an apathetic state to angry outbursts to fighting and even murder. The very desperate and drastic actions that people take when they are triggered by intense emotions are done for the release or the relief of these painful feelings.

Whether these actions are taken on impulse or premeditation, it is done to release the intense, negative emotions to feel a relief. In other words, it's done to feel better.

We would like to believe that we can and should always have control over our actions, but this is much easier said than done and for some people it's an impossibility.

Even in cases where crimes are premeditated and carefully planned, are done in an effort to get relief.

The reason why most will disagree with this is because we've spent a whole lifetime not understanding just how deeply intense and desperate the need for emotional relief is.

For some people even hurting people physically, bullying, stealing, and raping feels like an involuntary process. Believe it or not, whatever people do, they honestly believe they must do it.

Most people believe that when human beings do bad things, it is because they are evil, and they could or should have avoided it. This is not actually the case.

Try to think about this as an important thing in your life that you believe you must do to make your life better. Can you just stop having this need? Even if you stop pursuing it, you cannot stop the feeling of needing it.

In this case, the needs are being pushed by extremely desperate, aggressive negative energies like fear, shame, anger etc.

When we feel hungry, thirsty, sick, no one questions, if we should fulfill these needs since if we don't, we may die. Well, the same applies to our emotional needs and egotistical needs.

The reason why we are living in such a dangerous world is that we have not taught the value of attending to our emotional needs in a healthy way. We were never taught that our emotional system is just as important as our physical bodies. We assume that our human intellect is advanced enough to always decide what actions we can control or not control.

~~~~*

You may ask. "Why did I go from speaking on the psychological aspects of the relationship between the police and "minorities to this previous topic?".

This analysis is for us to understand how all humans function, from the police to the convict to everyone in between.

Police officers, who have bad intentions towards minorities, do act on their desperate, needy negative emotions but don't forget about the ones who may mean well but are pushed to the limit.

What I'm trying to convey here is that every need we have is valid, whether it's an emotional need or a physical need. They are all equally powerful and must be fulfilled. And so, we must see that every action, taken from having desperate needs are also valid.

You may be a person who didn't have to live a life that created extremely strong negative emotional energies and because of this, you don't have the height of volatility that some other people have.

When some people feel strongly about something, it becomes normal and natural for them to act out in a violent rage. The energies that are influencing their actions are too painful, powerful, and intense to be controlled, so hurting people verbally, emotionally or physically is how they must relieve themselves from the pain.

I like to explain this concept like this: people aren't bad, they just aren't emotionally able to not be violent. It's just like anything in your life that is automatic or even inevitable.

The way you deal with someone who vandalized your car might be less aggressive than someone else. Not because this other person is inherently bad or evil. But because he was brought up in an environment that nurtured him in a way that, when combined with other aspects of his personality, causes his reaction to have a natural, emotional, automatic flow that results in violent behavior.

Everyone, from a thug, gang member, serial killer to a mass murderer, takes actions that they believe they must take.

A police officer is no different, whether good or bad, he believes that he must do what he does.

This is not to say that the negative actions taken by police officers are to be tolerated or overlooked. This is an explanation as to why and how humans end up becoming something that most people deem as unacceptable by society's standards.

Every Human is an individual consciousness that has physical and non-physical body parts that also have their own consciousness, which carries their own needs.

The needs your physical body parts have is nutrition from healthy foods. The nutrition your emotions need is fulfillment and satisfaction.

Your ego doesn't know how to fulfill itself from pure positivity, so it gets its satisfaction in a negative way.

None of these needs is more valid than the other. They are just different, is functioning, and are expressed differently. Your non-physical needs are just expressed using thoughts, emotions, feelings, ego, fear etc.

They should never be taken for granted, ignored, underestimated, or confused for sinful, evil, "un-relatable" things that lead to avoidable actions.

This may sound as if I am saying that if someone needs to kill, then he should. No;

What I'm actually saying is, the need exists, and it can't just go away. So, people will act on them. But the reason these people take violent actions is that nobody showed them how to introduce something different and positive to the need, to cause a shift from the impulses of violent behavior.

This concept is not easy to accept. It's not easy for the mind that has been programmed for years to only understand from a one-dimensional standpoint to grasp such a "remote" concept.

s In this life, we are deeply in-tuned in our logical mind, which likes to decide between real or unreal, possible or impossible, practical or impractical; along with the conditioning of right versus wrong. These things combined, caused our brains to close off from the flow of consciousness that could open to a concept like this or at least give it some credence.

For now, this will just seem like subjective philosophy, though it is an objective truth.

CHAPTER 8

BLM

A perceived unfair acquittal of George Zimmerman in 2013, who shot and killed a teen named Trayvon Martin in 2012, gave rise to a new social movement social movement called Black Lives Matter. This movement was given strong media attention during the protests of the killing of two men in 2014, Michael Brown in Ferguson Missouri and Eric Garner in New York.

It was organized originally in the Black American community but is supported by members of other races and nationalities. Never before had a movement been so widely embraced. People from all cultures and classes, pooled in to support what they believe, was a cause for Freedom and equality. But is it freeing people? Is it causing equality?

Every generation has had its share of political problems and like always, people who are affected by these issues, gather to protest, but has protesting alone ever cause true change?

Political problems do not begin on a political level. Every political issue is first an emotional issue. It is each person's psychological and emotional problems accumulate to form one collective social affair.

Protesting does two main things. 1. It seeks to get attention from the authorities to make rules to stop people from doing bad things. 2. It may cause people to stop or slow down on doing bad things, out of fear of being penalized or punished by the justice system. Neither of these will actually lead to true, positive change.

If these social problems, boils down to each individual's mental, emotional issues, then protesting will never actually create the results we are looking for. Protesting may create a temporary ease of conflict, but the same issues will spring up again because the ease was just people choosing to "chill out." Someone or something will cause the very problem to be triggered and again we are dealing with the same issues.

There will be a great probability of similar problems to come back because the emotional root of the issue was never resolved.

Getting the government to pass laws against hate crimes won't fix the problems. There can be no resolution without the understanding that it all starts with "SELF." THIS IS A SELF WORK PROCESS that laws, rules, and government cannot single-handedly fix from their offices.

These lawmakers are humans themselves that also, unknowingly carry the very mental maladies that contribute to the bigger political crisis. We look to the authorities to solve our problems, yet they are a part of the problem.

A social movement like Black Lives Matter is set up to ask the government to create policies that demands the police and non-blacks to stop killing, de-valuing and degrading black people.

The people in the movement come out in their numbers and gather with their signs in hopes of getting the authorities to hear their voices and enforce rules that will stop black people from being shot. But how would this work?

How could the people in the government stay in their offices and prevent something from happening in communities all over a landmass that spreads 3.797 million square miles?

When have laws and strict guidelines ever stopped anyone from committing crimes?

There is no way to know who is capable of doing bad things. Most humans aren't intuitive enough to know if someone is capable of criminal activities just by looking at them.

For anything to work, the Government would have to allow each member of the population to have their own personal live-in police officer to monitor their every move for twenty-four hours a day. Then these police officers will need their own police officers.

Demanding the government to create restrictions to prevent murder can never work. It is not up to the government or any system to end a "people issue" that boils down to an individual level. This is like asking the government to pass laws to fix everyone's Anxiety.

People have been using protests for decades to persuade the system to change their policies and create social change. When it comes to racism, this approach has never really worked. Because if so, we wouldn't still be facing the challenges that we are today.

Depending on what is being pursued, the attempt may be somewhat effective; most of the time a public demonstration will serve to alter the current political climate, only on a small surface level.

Does "Black Lives Matter," Matters?

In my opinion, most social movements are counterproductive. Here is why:

Whenever you begin to fight any system, it will be fighting you back. People would not be fighting unless they really believe they have to, which means they also believe they have to win. People who have to win will never give up their fight. Therefore, the fight will go on and grow bigger until it becomes physical and may escalate into a war. Even when the physical war is over, the fight itself is not over because the mental/emotional root was not cleared up.

The more you fight against something the more it fights against you, then it increases and creates a higher possibility of you losing the fight.

The most important part of this is, when you force and shame people into making a change, they won't actually change. They will just consciously become selective with their words and attitudes to appease the politically correct social movement.

Now, there is more than one reason why the Social movement "Black Lives Matter" is flawed. There are other unconscious dangerous and potentially deadly issues involved here that most people aren't catching on to.

~~~~*

Most people are stuck on the conscious level of their minds. Both the subconscious and the conscious minds have layers within them. "Black lives matter" is a conscious mind statement with a surface purpose for conscious/surface benefits. However, it is a conscious statement with a subconscious/subliminal message.

Black people more than any other people, have lived for centuries in an unawareness and denial of how they view themselves. Most people wouldn't realize what years of slavery can do to a people's sense of worth, even generations after. And even after slavery, the abuse continued.

Just like a child who is being abused by someone, the self-perception of this child, will be significantly poor, desperate, and needy. For Black people, the poor sense of self takes many forms. It will play out in their personalities as aggression, violence, despair, vulgarity, "subnormal" conduct, subservience, self-abuse, misfortune, poverty etc.

The general disposition of any being who carries a weak sense of self will be one that lacks value.

The way you think, and feel is the way you will act and live, plus the way you treat yourself will be the way other people treat you.

Therefore, if some black people carry themselves in a negative way and treat each other and their community poorly, then the natural flow of life says that others will respond to black people in the same way.

Most black people would feel much pride to say that they don't feel good about who they are as a race. And even when they are consciously aware of this self-perception, they wouldn't openly declare it, because they believe it will make them look weak. But the truth will be displayed in their actions and living conditions.

This is where a major flaw with the statement "black lives matter comes in.

The reason this statement exists and is being repeated over and over via the media and the public is because this is something that is not believed by black people or non-black people. Black people don't value their own lives and so others cannot give you what you can't give to yourself.

When people, in general, believe that they are supposed to be good and strong, if they can't display it with their actions, they will compensate by saying with their words. If we can't practice it, we will preach it. Hence, "BLACK LIVES MATTER!".

Black people believe that they have to say things that are uplifting and positive about themselves and their community because of a fear of being judged. The truth that they actually believe about themselves is wronged and condemned by the black community. So now, they have to say the opposite of what they truly feel. The truth is pushed down into their subconscious minds and stays there.

Now, remember that the way you treat yourself, will be the way others treat you and respond to you. Non-black people will not value black people's lives because so many black people are living in a space of lacking value. Which brings up another truth, that non-black people too are forced to lie to themselves about how they feel about black people while expressing the politically correct terms. They force themselves to follow along with this requirement because of the desperate need to be seen as "not racist." So, both blacks and non-blacks have suppressed their true feelings about the way they feel about black people and they both only expressed what is expected of them. Still, the truth lingers deep within the subconscious aspects of their being.

Most of what people express with their words are the things that are "right", and these are the things they have on the conscious level of the mind. The subconscious is packed with all the thoughts and beliefs that they truly believe but are condemned.

This is telling us that "Black lives Matter" has a double meaning. Black lives matter has good intentions, but it is deriving from unhealthy subconscious beliefs. The good intentions are on the conscious mind level and the unhealthy beliefs are hidden deep within the subconscious mind.

The truth within DOUBLE MEANING STATEMENTS like "Black Lives Matter," will be received and understood on the mind levels that they resonate with.

When People hear the words "BLACK LIVES MATTER!", their Conscious minds understands the conscious meaning of this multi-conscious statement to mean that Black People are just as important as everyone else. However, the statement (Black Lives Matter) does have an unintentional subliminal message. So, a higher level of everyone's subconscious minds says "I'm not sure how I feel but I want to stand up for what is right."

For non-black People, a deeper level of their subconscious asks " If they really believe this would they be announcing it?

While the even deeper suppressed truth says things like, "I don't love these people, I don't want to be around these people, I don't like things about these people, I prefer my own people, etc.

For Black People, their deepest subconscious truth is " I don't value my life, I don't value my own people, I feel like I don't matter, I feel less than others.

When "BLM" is heard all of the suppressed truth on all levels are activated at the same time, then the hidden truth becomes somewhat more conscious. The Words triggers and activate the Deepest Darkest Subconscious Truth, which influences the conscious mind.

Now ask yourself this question. If you really believe something to be true, would you need to shout it to others? Really, think about this. If you truly believe your life has value, would you need to say it? This is not something you say, this is an innate knowing that you'd have or that you should have. You would live it out naturally and effortlessly, if it was something you really believed.

There is a reason why nobody goes around shouting just how valuable diamonds are. Nobody screams "Diamonds matter" because most people are very much aware of the value that diamonds have in society. If I should start to shout, "Diamonds matter, Diamonds matter!" The first thing people will do is, question the value of diamonds, because a part of their minds knows that if diamonds are valuable, then it will be true for everyone.

This is the very mental transaction that occurs between Black Lives Matter, and the public.

When people see and hear the statement "Black Lives Matter", a certain aspect of their minds knows that if this were something that black people really believed, and then they wouldn't have to say it.

This multi-layered mind activation and transfer are causing the suppressed belief that black lives does not matter to be reinforced, reactivated and resurfaced. Once we have reinforced this belief, it is strengthened in the minds of blacks and non-blacks.

The other important thing to understand is that our consciousness will and can only allow us to live the truth of what we feel. The truth is the most powerful and impactful aspects of you. We may try to say what is expected and what is PC, but our actions and some of our non-verbal expressions will demonstrate the truth.

This only means that the reinforcement of the truth of how black lives are perceived will only result in more racism, more discrimination, more hatred, more racially motivated crimes and even more "black on black crimes".

We need to understand that these "small" things, we see as "just words" aren't just words because every decision, every move, every action is existing first as a thought, beliefs, feelings, and emotions.

There is not one action you can take that was not first a thought. Whether the action was quick, impulsive, or premeditated.

For the most part, the subconscious mind is where the truth of "black lives does not matter" lives and the truth will have a much stronger influence on our minds and actions.

When we tell the world that "Black Lives Matter," we actually send the opposite message because if this were true for Blacks, they would live it, instead of saying it.

It is a natural and automatic process for people to treat you the way you treat yourself. This is a truth that will be true whether you've accepted it or not, and the truth will come out in some form, emotionally, verbally, physically and either directly or indirectly.

When people say "Black Lives matter," what they are doing is trying to convince themselves and others of something they want to believe and not something they actually do believe.

Overall, this movement had good intentions, but it is totally working against its purpose. Not only is this movement "not" helping but also it is actually creating more of the very problems it originally intended to solve.

BLACK LIVES MATTER KILLS!

I had created other content on this very topic with these very points, but I just get the feeling that people do not understand the severity of this situation.

What I am saying is, the movement called BLACK LIVES MATTER is causing and will cause more black people to die at the hands of racist cops and civilians. As in literal KILLINGS/ MURDERS/ DEATHS. "YES THAT!"

Please do not take this lightly.

Please remember that every action was first a thought. Every negative, violent thing that people do exists first as a thought. So, if the subliminal thought that is involved with the movement Black Lives Matter is "black lives does not matter", then this thought will lead to action, events and occurrences that "shows", black lives does not matter.

Swapping Perspectives?

Like a "junkie" who is dirty on the street, he does not value himself enough to get clean on any level, so people will not give him the human respect that he wants. Think about a prostitute who goes around, giving her body to anyone who will pay. Most of the times a prostitute does not value her body and so people will treat and give her the same value that she gives herself.

If you're a black person reading this passage, you may interpret this as victim blaming. But can you say that you would give a junkie or a prostitute the utmost respect as other "decent" human beings? Can you honestly say that you see or treat people who behave a certain way, as you would treat the "nice" and clean people? If you can't actually do this, how could you expect others to do it?

That junkie or prostitute, (just like you) would like to be treated with honor and respect. Believe it or not, they actually desire it and most times, they don't understand why they don't get respect (just like you). You can go ahead and test it yourself, and you will see that no matter how hard you try, you will never be able to do that for them, as your conscious mind says, "no way", I can't respect that".

You only know that this person "does not deserve" your respect based on your personal moral standards.

If you could agree that there are types of folks that you respect less than others, then maybe you could see how it's possible that some people won't respect you. Maybe you could understand how you may be the type of person that some people may not respect or value.

You may say, "well I'm not a junkie or a prostitute; it's not fair to compare my race to a "junkie-ism" and prostitution. "I can't help my race." "Not respecting someone because of their race is not a valid reason to not respect someone."

For non-black people, from the outside looking in, the black community as a whole will seem like it's filled with images that represent despair, degeneration, and dysfunction.

You as a black individual may not epitomize the images of dysfunction and degeneracy that exists within the black community, but people's minds will register the negative things they see some black people do as "the norm," especially if these negative things are done over and over by black people. Therefore, you as a black individual may get lumped into one negative category, just like you expect all prostitutes and junkies to always be a certain way.

I am not comparing black people to prostitutes and junkies, I am just using this as an analogy for you to understand that the general way you perceive and treat a certain kind of people, is similar to how others may perceive and treat you.

The negative ways in which the black community is commonly perceived, is an accurate perception but not for every person in the black community.

People outside of the black community do not have enough natural interest in the black community to dissect it and decide who is "good" versus bad. When humans set themselves apart from a particular group of people, their minds will only or mostly be fixated on the goodness of the people in their own community. There is hardly any interest in recognizing the positivity of the other groups. Instead, they will dwell on the negative aspects of the other group(s) because the human mind is generally more intrigued by negativity. The human ego (mind) also needs this perceived negativity to feel better about itself and its own group.

This self-interest also tells the ego to highlight the negative aspects of others as a reminder of why they should continue to separate and segregate from them. This process also explains one reason why the mind tends to generalize.

This is how whites, blacks and everyone else gets stereotyped through generalization. White people aren't the only people who generalizes. We all do it because we all function the same in many ways.

Based on this natural process of our psyche, we will place value on different groups of people, according to our general perception of their conduct. Their lives will matter to the degree of which we perceive their worth.

Black Identity Politics

We see minority groups, especially blacks practicing different kinds of identity politics. Some of us find it problematic and others see no harm in it.

Black identity politics started a long time ago and existed as a response to the oppression from White supremacy and White identity politics.

After a while, White identity politics was forbidden and condemned while black identity politics and black pride was not and sometimes even encouraged.

Now some members of the white community saw this as unfair and a double standard that was being enabled by the media and the government. While this may be true, there is no way that Black identity politics could openly exist, if White identity politics didn't exist on some level.

White people were and are still involved in their own identity politics; they just didn't express it aloud. Whites (including the "nice, liberal" Whites) were still very separatist without saying that they were, and so Black people continued with their Black pride as a response to the negative effects of White's covert and unconscious identity politics.

This White identity politics was both covert/overt and covert/unconscious. Covert/overt means that there were still white people who were overt racists/White supremacists but was operating underground for a while. Covert/unconscious refers to the white people who say and do the "right," politically correct things but were still very racist and separatist on a subconscious level.

The interesting part of being a covert racist is that you will carry out very small and subtle discriminatory and separatist actions without knowing you are doing it. People will recognize this in some way and respond aggressively.

In this case, black people have caught sight of this subtle racism and continued to respond with their own identity politics just in the opposite way (i.e. overt).

Black people's identity politics and pride is rooted in deep victimhood. Black people don't know this because on the surface it seems like the opposite of victimhood. Black identity politics and pride is only a disguise for weaknesses.

Now here's the truth about the human mind. Both the conscious and the subconscious layers of the mind is interpreting the truth of any situation. So, when we are dealing with victimhood, it will be interpreted as victimhood, whether it is obvious or if it's disguised as strength and pride. Moreover, the mind is seeing it as a weakness whether we are consciously aware of that or not.

Once the mind has a perception of you (conscious or subconscious) it will and has to interact and treat you the way it perceives you. Meaning that white people will perceive black pride/identity politics as victimhood and weakness and the interaction and exchanges between blacks and whites will continue to be that of the victim and perpetrator (or perceived perpetrator).

When you operate from a weak place it will be received as weakness, it will create more situations and occurrences where you are weakened and victimized. You will continue to experience more discrimination, more isolation, more separation, and even more abuse.

Identity politics is dangerous for more reasons than one. You cannot invest so much identity in your race without creating even more separation. It's true that we all identify with our races but when there is so much emphasis; being deliberately placed on being black (and blackness), it causes people to only see you for your blackness. It takes away from making a true connection with people because they can't get past your "blackness" to get to you. You cannot blame it all on them when you do it to yourself. The way you treat yourself will be the way others treat you.

If people cannot get past your blackness, then their positive and negative, perception and response to you will be related to your race, i.e. "Racist." If everything about you, involves your race, this is the message that you send to people. Their minds will be too crowded with thoughts of your blackness, that it becomes impossible for them to connect with you on any other level.

<u>What else does identity politics do?</u>

It causes everyone to indulge in identity politics. In present day, black identity politics has become very aggressive, very abrasive, and a bit irrational. While their feelings and views are valid, I cannot ignore just how pervasive this Identity politics is, and how it has influenced other people to be the same way.

This was inevitable because Black identity politics involves blaming White people.

A great deal of anger is created within people who are being blamed. When you blame others, you are telling them that they have to carry the responsibility for your problems and your pain. This leads to people feeling pressured and therefore powerless. What do we know now about powerlessness? it triggers the kind of fear that leads to anger.

Black identity politics also involves a kind of open, raw, unapologetic black pride. Black pride influences White pride. Now mix the anger from blame with this new wave of White pride and this is a sure recipe for a "war monger mentality" among whites. No wonder, in today's world, there is a rise of the White Nationalism and the Alt-right movement.

~~~~*

We are so desperately afraid of "victim blaming" even when it's not actually victim blaming.

Steering away from showing the victims how they are contributing to their own problems will never solve anything.

Accept it or not, the victims have a big role to play in fixing the problems in their lives. The "non-victims" and "perpetrators" are less affected by these problems so their motivation to help is not as strong.

Why would the "perpetrators," give up their position of dominance to be less dominant?

Identity, within itself, causes people to separate from each other. When you add the politics to it, the separation is even stronger. This is extremely dangerous for society because when people separate with identity, they also disconnect from each other.

The natural state of any living being is to care for one another primarily because they see themselves in each other. This is what connection is.

When humans disconnect, they can no longer see themselves in each other, therefore, making it easy for them to hurt one another, both emotionally and physically. If I can't see myself in you then I can hurt you, as your hurt is your hurt and not mine.

If we are separated, then we can't connect; connection is what we use to see the value in each other.

CHAPTER 9

Solutions

For years on top of years, we have been stuck in a dangerous cycle, where the worldwide problem of racism is concerned. I believe we stay stuck for more than just a few reasons, but there are two main things that I see standing in between us and a possible post-racist society. These are:

1. We make being racist, the absolute worst thing in the world (we make it wrong for someone to be racist).

2. Being unaware that racism is a psycho-emotional issue first.

These two issues have further resulted in two other major problems:

1. People hiding and suppressing their racist feelings because, if racism is the worst thing in the world, then "my racist feelings make me the worst person in the world."

2. People expecting the government to solve racism, from believing it's a social/political issue first instead of a psycho/emotional issue first.

~~~~*

Every so often, a famous person is caught saying and or doing something politically incorrect. If it's related to race, you can bet, that famous person will be taken down from the height of stardom that they had climbed to in their long-running career. Society totally destroys this celebrity's life, career and sometimes even their finances are affected, because all the big sponsors and co-operations decide to pull out of "that major deal."

The race or group that were affect by the celeb's words, make it their duty to let society know just how adamant they are about having this person lose their celebrity status. They want "him" removed from the public's eye because he was wrong for saying what he said.

To say that this method of disciplining celebrities is flawed, is a colossal size understatement, because not only is it flawed but it is also one of the very things that is causing racism to be spiraling down to hell as we speak. This course of action is the pinnacle of detriment where racism is concerned.

This is a problem because it tells people in society, that being racist is the absolute worst thing to be and if you are; your life will be destroyed.

Political Correctness within itself has done a great job in getting people to suppress the truth and lie to themselves, now we have added more to plenty by destroying people's lives when they choose to let out what's going on inside of them. Now everyone is on this super self-guard where they have to walk on a chalk line, trying to be careful around others.

Think about something. If someone said something racist, what is that telling us? It's telling us that this person is releasing something that already exists inside of him. If it exists inside of him, it's going to come out of him.

So, when we shut him up and shut him down, we have not accomplished anything. What actually happened is he will only continue to trap those feelings inside his mind.

If they are trapped inside of him then he has not stopped being racist. Not only that, if this person is racist against black people (for example), destroying his celebrity/financial privilege will probably make him even more racist, because he's already a "racist" and now the people he hates his "causing" him to lose everything, so now he hates them even more.

You may say, "Well he caused it on himself, he shouldn't have said that." While I understand this point, his mind will not process it like that. You have to remember that the ego/mind has to be right and even when people are "wrong" they have to find someone else to blame. Therefore, if someone loses their TV show because of making derogatory remarks about black people, as far as his mind is concerned, black people did this to him.

He will not be the only one whose racist feelings will heighten because of this. It's also the people in the population who think like him and also the white people who believe that all political correct policies should be done away with. If you ask me, I believe that this course of action does anger the majority white people, whether they admit it or not.

Why is this a problem? Because just like I stated in a previous chapter, the anger from things like this, is a big part of what turns people into war mongers. And also, white people would most likely be the ones to initiate a race war.

I am not saying that people should say negative racial things in the media; however, the way these situations are currently being dealt with, is sending a dangerous message to the public.

There are things that need to be said that may unpleasant to the ear, but they have to be said so people could understand the truth. Which takes me to my next point that, the most important thing about what is being said is the intentions behind the words.

If we set the intention to have a productive discussion, even if there are hurtful words being exchanged, it will not hurt as bad as when someone is definitely trying to hurt you. You have to trust yourself to know the difference, which is not hard because we all can intuitively sense when someone is being passive aggressive versus when someone is trying to make a productive point.

Now sometimes these celebrities do have negative intentions behind the things they say but this is where we have to let these celebs understand that the reason they want to hurt others is because they themselves are hurting. Once they fully understand this truth, they will be more interested in changing and releasing the emotions associated with the hurt that causes them to want to hurt others verbally.

The kind of punishment that is currently being used for people and celebrities who say racially disparaging things, is a way of scaring the nation into becoming "psychotically" PC and it heightens the belief that racism and being racist is the worst thing in the world.

~~~~*

A strong stance of this book is that all human beings are prejudiced and racist. If all of these human beings who are racist, continues to believe that "a racist" is the worse person in the world, they will:

1. Continue to lie to themselves about being racist.
2. As a result, hide and stuff down the truth. As I may have said before, this will only cause the racist feelings to heighten.

When the mind is fighting the truth, it is giving it a lot of focus energy and whatever you focus on will grow in your mind. Just like when you are studying for a test, you focus so much on the information that it becomes stronger in your mind.

Now imagine, millions of people doing this in one country (and the entire world) at one time. You don't have to do much imagining because this is actually what we've been living in real life. Moreover, this is one main reason why we are currently in the political state that we are.

When we are dealing with racism, we are dealing with people's thoughts, beliefs, and feelings about another people, which mean we are dealing with a psychological and emotional issue. The negative beliefs that create our racist feelings in our bodies are related to our negative emotions.

The way to release negative emotions and beliefs is by first acknowledging them.

This is why it's important to throw out the concept that being racist is the most horrible thing to be. If society continues to cast out the people who openly say racist things, then nobody will acknowledge their racist feelings inside of them. The feelings will stay inside of everyone, festering and growing until we get to a state where everything as escalated to the point of no control. (Which we are almost at this point).

To cure any issue, there has to be the acknowledgment. If you have Kidney disease, you have to first acknowledge the disease to move towards methods of healing. Telling yourself that you don't have Kidney disease, will not cause the disease to go away. We first have to acknowledge the things we are thinking and believing first, to take the next steps to release it from our minds.

This concept of acknowledgment being the first step to healing, works with almost everything in our lives, but it is especially true when dealing with non-physical energies like emotions.

The acknowledgment of our racist feelings and belief is the first step to healing ourselves from racism. This may not seem like much, but once you've done this you have accomplished half of the self-work needed.

It's amazing how we expect the same old, overused methods of managing racism to work. We see that over the years they have never really worked but we still continue to use them.

It usually plays out like this: A hate crime has occurred; Black people are outraged by it. They take to the street to protest, they call on some well-known civil rights activists and start a Social Justice Movement. They keep protesting until maybe the justice system create some tighter laws and policies to get the "hate criminals" to think twice about committing hate crimes.

This is the usual approach. This has been the procedure since day one, yet in today's world the racial tension is growing more and more.

Society expects the government to do something about racism so the government as well as civil organization joins forces to do the only and best things, they believe will or can help.

<u>Forcing people to integrate?</u>

Another counter-productive measure that the system always uses is forcing integration onto people. This is bad, because if people are not willing to integrate, then it means that they are not ready.

If we force people to integrate when they don't want to, it will create more collective resentment and, therefore, more division.

When people are forced to do something that makes them uncomfortable, they will hate the thing that's causing the discomfort even more.

Every time they see the people whom they are being forced to integrate with, they are reminded of why they hate them in the first place, then there comes the discomfort of being forced. This makes the resentment stronger.

It's best to allow people to do what they prefer to do and what makes them comfortable, while helping them to heal from the hatred that inspires separation. By doing this, people will feel a sense of freedom and eventually feel a natural need to connect with each other, thereby influencing integration.

None of the above strategies has ever or will ever solve racism. These are not only counter-productive, but they are only surface methods that only appeal to the conscious mind. This is a problem because most of the mental emotional issues that are driving racism are subconscious.

If you read this book up to this point you may notice that most of the chapters ended on the very concept that most of what is keeping racism alive is living on the subconscious mind of society as a collective. We cannot use shallow, "on the surface" methods to solve a mostly subconscious issue.

We need to go deeper. Sink below the surface. Get out of the boat and get into the submarine.

~~~~*

I hope that I was able to use the points in the previous chapters of this book to impact your mind to the point where you are at least "somewhat" in agreement that this problem is mostly subconscious, and we have to search deeper to find the truth.

<u>So how do we actually solve the issue of Race within the USA and the world?</u>

There are billions of people in the world, all of which are racist to some degree.

There is no way you can change a person's emotions. There is no way to go inside of someone's body and change the way they way feel, and there is most certainly, no possible way the Government could pass laws that could change people's feelings and beliefs.

We cannot change people. People have to work on changing themselves. If they want to, because for each individual to change, they have to want to make that change, which is another important reason for society to make it less "evil" to be racist. No one will want to change if they know that admitting to being racist makes them evil and could cause them to be ostracized or punished.

One very interesting thing about human beings is, when they see everyone trying to make a change, they will want to jump on board. But it will start with you. You are the one who will be the leader among your friends and your tribe, who will inspire them to turn a new page.

~~~~*

Racism will always boil down to beliefs and emotions which means it's mostly an individual issue. Therefore, each individual will have to take responsibility for their own thoughts, feelings, and beliefs, in order for society to see any change as far as racism goes. It is not up to the government, it's up to us. Solving racism will mean that each individual will have to take steps to shift their consciousness and make a conscious effort to acknowledge the truth inside of them.

Now what does this mean for racism in our society? It means there is no overnight remedy for racism.

HOWEVER: There are certain steps we can take towards our personal experiences that can ultimately reduce any suffering related to race and race relations in the Society. These methods are designed to lessen most of the fears and anxiety involved with people's interactions with each other, and after while of applying these things we may wake up one day and say that racism is gone from our lives (or mostly gone). However, this is where we have to start.

I am providing different processes, techniques, and exercises that are designed to help each individual to free themselves from the pain of carrying around racist feelings within them. This is the first and only step towards creating a stronger future for our world.

The Different Steps include:

* How to release racist feelings by acknowledging your own racism.

* Things to consider and things to think about that can help to shift your consciousness towards open-mindedness, where it will be easier to understand yourself, your needs and to understand other people.

* Techniques to reprogram the mind and to help change negative beliefs about other races and groups; you will be re-programming your mind to believe more positive things in regard to race, by making focus lists. This may seem trivial, but it is a very powerful way to get the mind to focus positively to create a different collective reality.

* Actual emotional exercises to release negative emotions associated with racist feelings that we have accumulated over the years.

<u>Please try to keep an open mind towards each process.</u>

These techniques are for all people, not just White people. If you are a black person who still believes that you can't be racist because you are black, just tell yourself that you will try out these healing methods regardless.

INTEREST IN HEALING HAS TO BE INVESTED ON BOTH SIDES, (WHICH INCUDES ALL PEOPLE OF COLOR).

NOTE: I SUGGEST THAT YOU USE ONLY ONE PROCEDURE AT A TIME. YOU CAN TRY EACH ONE DAILY, WEEKLY, BI-WEEKLY, OR MONTHLY. DONT RUSH YOURSELF. FEEL FREE TO MOVE ON TO ANOTHER, WHEN YOU ARE READY OR WHEN YOU BELIEVE YOU'VE ACHIEVED THE RESULT YOU NEEDED FROM THE CURRENT ONE.

NOTE: ALL PEOPLE, SHOULD DO, AND TAKE PART IN THESE PRACTICES, NOT JUST THE PEOPLE WHO ARE "THE KNOWN RACISTS" OR HIGHLY RACIST. REMEMBER, ALL HUMANS ARE RACIST; SOME ARE JUST MORE RACIST THAN OTHERS ARE.

Again, acknowledgment is key.

Acknowledging any negative energy in your body will start the healing process for you. It is the first level of release.

I would suggest for all human beings to say two main things to start their personal healing of their own racist feelings and beliefs.

1. Stand in from of a mirror and say, "I AM A RACIST, I AM ACKNOWLEDGING THIS AND ALLOWING THIS MOMENT TO BE THE INITIAL STAGE OF MY HEALING PROCESS, AND AS OF TODAY I WILL ALWAYS ACKNOWLEDGE MY RACIST FEELINGS".

2. "I AM SETTING MY INTENTION TO TAKE STEPS TOWARDS HEALING MY SELF FROM RACIST THOUGHTS, BELIEFS, AND FEELINGS, AND THE METHODS THAT I USE WILL GRADUALLY RELEASE THE RACIST ENERGIES FROM MY MIND AND BODY".

What you are doing here is setting an official intention to always recognize and acknowledge our racist feelings, going forward.

You should also, always set your intention when you are about to use one of my emotional self-help exercises for racism, set this intention to release any energy/emotion associated with being prejudice/racist/bigoted.

Now that you have set your official intention to commit to your progress, there are two other important things for you to do to initiate your healing process.

1. The Racist Work Sheet.

I created a worksheet ("The Racist feeling worksheet") that I placed towards the ending of this chapter. This is a continuation of the acknowledgment process. It also involves other important "self-work" methods to help you release these racist energies within your being. I suggest that you go to the end of this chapter to locate this work sheet and work on it NOW. Then come back right HERE to the next step. (You can create copies of your worksheet, to continue working on yourself and also to use it regarding the various races of people that affect you negatively).

2. Venting

- Set your intension to release negative emotions related to race, before you do this exercise.

I want you to vent about everything that bothers you about race and racism in society, the people you are racist towards and the people who are racist towards you. You can vent with your words or do it in writing form. Vent about the race of people that bothers you the most. Say everything that is on your mind without trying to be nice or politically correct. Be as mean as you feel. Please do not hold back. Let it all out at once. Be as aggressive as you can.

I would suggest that you use something like a punching bag or a pillow to punch, hit, and kick on. You can also try out using a baseball bat or a long piece of wood to destroy old used objects like bags, bottles, old furniture, garbage etc. as long as you are not physically harming yourself, other people or animals, or plants.

Use this approach while spewing all the things that frustrates you. Even if the things you are saying are extremely selfish or narcissistic, say everything you feel and believe about yourself, your race, about other races and race politics in this society.

Keep going until you feel a very strong relief and almost like you literally have no more words left related to the people and situation that you hate.

Immediately after you are done, take three of the deepest, largest breaths that you have ever taken in your life. When you breathe out, just know that you are breathing out, even more negative energy, and tension associated with your racist feelings.

Note: If you believe venting is a good way to release your racist feelings, you can do it whenever you need to or whenever racial issues has troubled you.

Once you've done the acknowledgment, set intension, Venting and the worksheet. Start living your truth by telling others all about your new outlook on racism, tell them about your true feelings, and tell them about the importance of acknowledging the truth. Tell them that you have racist feelings and you believe all people do. Tell them that they are not bad people; they are only humans that exist with both negative and positive beliefs and feelings.

Also, tell them that you are working on these feelings and they can too. Let them know of the inner peace you have acquired from taking this path; tell them that this path is also their path; they are doing it for their own emotional health and peace of mind, and not for anyone else's.

By doing this, you are giving people the freedom and the permission to release their racist feelings by being truthful. This is how you do your part in changing the world because the people you help in this way will help others and soon the whole Globe will be on board with this movement and together we will create a whole new World.

- After you do these first four things try out the following techniques that I've provided to continue the healing process.

~~~~*

One major factor that causes conflict in this society is our disagreements. The things we stand for, are related to the issues that affect us. These issues means a lot to us, and we have strong desperate feelings attached to these things. And these issues are different for different people.

We also need our side or our group to be right. We want to be right and we want the others to see that we are right. We also want people to see and understand our positions and struggles for what they are.

We want all these things while not realizing that we can't do these things ourselves. We cannot do these things for other people.

One way to deal with this mindset is to simply consider certain points.

Here are some thought exercises. I.e. things to consider and things to think about: <u>Please apply these mind practices to Racism</u>

<u>Mind Practice: A</u>

- Remember to always set the intention to release negative energy/emotions before all exercises and procedures.

The following practice is mainly for black people and "minorities" in general, White people can do it too but it's mostly for "minorities" because of the belief that "White people hate us for no reason."

- We all have at least one race, ethnicity, or group of people that we either hate, resent, or dislike. You would be hard-pressed to find an individual who absolutely love every type of people on the planet.

Even if that person exists, he will have at least one individual that he doesn't love.

- I want you to think about a group of people (except for white people) that you do not like. It doesn't have to be a race, it could be a gender or a mixture of race and gender, e.g. you may not like Mexican Men, or it could be Black Women.

- If you are still fixed on believing that you are not prejudiced against any group, well, do not think about a group. You can just think about one person in your life that you have some level of resentment towards.

- Now, try as hard as you can to like these people or person. Try to love them. Just decide to love them.

You will find that no matter what you do or how hard you try, you cannot just decide to like or love them. You cannot just like something you don't like. Contrary to popular belief, liking or loving someone is not based on a decision.

- Now, ask yourself this. If I have someone that I don't like, could it be, that the way I feel about these people (or person), is the way in which others feel about me or my people? For example, if you are a Black American person who hates or dislikes Black people from Haiti. Ask yourself, could the way I feel about Haitians, be the very way White Americans feel about me and other Black people?

- Now, think about these same people or person again. Have they ever put you in slavery? Did they wage war against your people? Did they ever use the government to systematically put you at a disadvantage in society?

(Please provide an answer to every question)

- This questioning, should make it easier for you to understand that you aren't very different from white people.

- It also makes you understand why people hold on certain negative feelings, because if you can't let go of yours, how could you expect others to let go of theirs.

- This method also helps you to see yourself in others and thus create grounds to build more understanding, empathy, solidarity, and connection.

Mind Practice: B

- Think about something that hurts you deeply, take a minute to notice how strong the hurt is that you are feeling. After that, think about something that hurts someone else. You will observe that you don't feel the same level of concern or stress about the other person's hurt, as you did about your own hurt feelings.

The level of pain that they are feeling is the same or maybe stronger than yours. But you can't feel theirs because you are in your own perspective and you are too concerned with your pain to feel anything for them.

- If you could understand that their problems are causing the same kind of pain as your problems is causing you, then you can see just how real, strong, and valid their concerns are and so you really can relate to their problems.

- You'll understand that they can't just change their minds about the hurt they feel, as you can't change your mind about the hurt you feel.

- You can't just get other people to care the same way you do about your issues, as you can't care for other people's problems the way you do about yours.

TECHNIQUES TO REPROGRAM THE MIND AND TRANSFORM NEGATIVE/RACIST BELIEFS.

- Before practicing this technique, set the intention to release negative emotions and beliefs associated with race.

Whatever you are feeling or believing will become a part of who you are. You cannot just get rid of something that is a part of you. If you try to fight that thing, you will not get rid of it. You will only get more of it because as I said before, when you fight something in your mind you are giving it a lot of focused energy, and whatever you focus on, you create more of.

If you fight, your Racist beliefs and feelings you will make them become a stronger force in your mind.

It's important to understand that there is no difference between suppressing your feelings and fighting your feelings. The suppression is a form of self-fight. What will actually work is the opposite.

I've found that it's best to positively acknowledge your feelings. We have to learn to approach negativity with the opposite of negativity if we want the cure for it.

I do recall saying that everything is energy. What we should know about every type of energy in this universe is that all energy will respond according to the energy you give to it. Give energy, negative energy and you'll get more negative energy, if you give energy, positive energy, then you'll get positive energy.

A dog is an energy form, if you fight a dog he will fight you back, and if you run away from a dog he will run after you.

Fire is energy, if you fight fire with more fire, you will get more fire. Humans are energy, if you try to fight the human, most times he will fight you back. Even if the human ("energy") don't fight you back physically, he will fight you in his mind. Either way it's still a fight and the principles still apply that what you fight will fight you back. And once it's fighting you, it's only building more of that energy that fights.

We have to administer positive energy to the negative energies in our lives. From a thought to a belief to our feelings.

The way to give our negative emotions and beliefs positive energy is by becoming accepting of them. We have to find approval for everything negative in our lives.

This is not a popular concept because for centuries, we have been existing in a society that, has been living by the "fight-fight back" rule. We do this with every aspect of our lives. Someone offends us, so we have to offend him or her. We watch this play out even on a governmental level, when a country attacks, the government send its military on a war mission to fight back that country. So, no wonder this concept extends to our minds and emotions.

In this life, most of what we believe has been taught to us in a backwards kind of fashion. This is why most of the outlooks and ideologies in this book seem so foreign because as a society, we got so use to the lie that the truth sounds outlandish.

~~~~*

I challenge you to try it out now, when you get a negative feeling from a negative thought, instead from responding with frustration and stress, just say to it, "there you are, I acknowledge you and I approve of you." Now watch how you feel immediately after. You should feel a quick flash of relief. In this case, the relief may not last for long because you have not been doing this practice for very long. But if you begin making this a regular practice, you will see how less stressful your life becomes.

There are a few techniques that I've chosen to share with you that will help you to find approval for the negative thoughts, beliefs, and emotions related to racist feelings and racism in general.

Exercise 1.

- Always set your intention to release negative emotions related to race, before you do this exercise.

If you have some hatred towards Mexicans; make a list of why its ok to feel this way. You may write it like this: (for example).

I hate Mexicans; this is ok because:

1. I can't just decide to stop hating them because it is not done by choice.

2. All my feelings are valid and happened as an automatic result of what I've experienced.

3. Because I am using different ways to release this hatred, so I will release all of it soon.

4. I am learning more and more to become ok with what I'm feeling.

5. Because if I fight the way I feel, it will only grow more.

6. All humans feel hatred sometimes.

7. I am not the only one that hates.

8. This feeling is coming from my dark side but its ok because I also have a light side.

*   Make this list as long as you can. Use points from my example list, only if it applies to your life. Read them over as often as possible.

You can also read them over whenever you feel your hatred and resentment are starting to re-emerge.

These are just some examples of what your list may look like. You are doing it to feel better and to become less prejudiced, so you have to work with even the thoughts that may be seen as dark. Don't be afraid to get as politically incorrect as possible. You are trying to release all the darkness inside of you, so holding back by trying to be nice or PC will only keep them trapped inside of you.

Some people may think this method is actually giving people to right to hate but this is not actually, how it works. The intention behind it is to release the negative beliefs and feelings, this intention will actually be the driving force that creates positive results.

Intention

When you set the intention to achieve a certain result, your mind/brain will believe the intention and everything you do relating to the situation stays with the intention. The end results are positive because the outcome followed the direction of the intention.

Focus creates more energy and the kind of focus will create the same kind energy. Acceptance is positive focus that creates positive results. Fighting is negative focus, which creates negative results. Now the intension behind the focus is what makes them different. So, because the intention of finding approval for hating Mexicans is positive, it will lead you to a positive place of feeling less hatred towards Mexicans. Therefore, even though it seems like a bad thing to be ok with hating someone, the good intention will create a completely different outcome.

Exercise 2.

-Write down negative things that you believe about a particular group of people. Then come up with at least one reason why it's ok for them to be this way.

- Always set your intention to release negative emotions related to race, before you do this exercise.

Example:

1. Black people are involved in gangs; it's ok because some of them had rough upbringings.

2. White people are "standoffish," it's ok because they don't understand my life.

Write down one whole list for one group of people, then move on to another group.

* Make these lists as long as you can. Use points from my example list, only if it applies to your life. Read them over as often as possible.

Exercise 3.

- Make a list of all the races and groups of people you resent or hate and then create a list for each group stating what makes these people wonderful and beautiful inside and out.

- Always set your intention to release negative emotions related to race, before you do this exercise.

Example:

Black People are wonderful because:

1. I've had good experiences with some of them, where they were very courteous.

2. They can be very nurturing.

3. They can be very spiritual.

4. They are very "soulful."

5. I like that they can be so artistic.

6. I've been around some black people who are extremely considerate and kind.

* Make this list as long as you can. Use points from my example list, only if it applies to your life. Read them over as often as possible.

-Make a list of how "these people" are just like us/me.

- Always set your intention to release negative emotions related to race, before you do this exercise.

Example:

White people are just like us because:

1. They want happy life like we do.

2. They want the best for them and their children just like we do.

3. We both have the same concerns and want the best for our community.

4. We both are trying to create success for our lives.

5. We both bleed red blood.

6. We both want to love and be loved.

* Make this list as long as you can. Use points from my example list, only if it applies to your life. Read them over as often as possible.

- Other important lists you should make are:

* How are we equal?

* How are we one? (I.e. one with your race and the races that you hate).

* Why/How "they" are not inferior to me.

* Make a list of all the times in your life that you actually have had positive/good experiences with the races/groups that you hate.

Please do not copy my lists word for word unless these items actually do pertain to your personal experiences with the particular group you choose to write about.

You can base these lists from your personal experiences and also the general perception but make sure the items on the list are true for you. Only write down things that you genuinely find to be positive or appealing. So, if

Black people being good dancers does not appeal to you (for whatever reason), then do not add that to your list.

Make as many of these lists as needed about the same group and also different groups. You can also become very specific about it; meaning you can do this exercise with religion, genders, sexuality, and even in a mixed form like "black women," Asian men, White men, Christian men, White Christians etc.

These exercises may not seem like they are going to be impactful but you will be surprise what happens to the mind once you start to feed it with the positive opposites; especially when you feed your mind by writing these things down. Somehow, writing causes the re-programming to truly register.

I suggest that you also read them over as often as you can, this way the re-programming truly sets in and will cause long term positive effects.

It is my number one desire to have as many people transform the negative beliefs in their minds regarding race so feel free to use any extra sources that you believe will help to shift your mind's consciousness regarding race. So, use your favorite Life Coach, Spiritual Teacher, Healer, Therapist, and Psychologists that you trust to help you. I would prefer that you choose sources that specialize in going into the subconscious mind. But if you are not getting real results please continue with the techniques in this book.

Techniques to discover the subconscious truth and also to release negative/Racist feelings and emotions.

- Remember to always set the intention to release negative energy/emotions.

If you really understood this book, you would know that one of the main messages being conveyed is that racist feelings has more to do with the hater than the people the hater hates. Most super racist haters will not agree, and even the ones who do agree, would not outwardly admit because of pride and also the fear of being seen as being wrong.

They are focused on the conscious reasons for hating so they won't see the truth of the issue because this truth is mostly lying dormant in their subconscious minds.

You can reveal the truth to yourself using procedures that are designed to pull out the subconscious truth. There are ways to discover the root and truth behind why you are racist and bigoted. When you discover the deep-rooted truth, it pulls the cover off the container that keeps the racist emotions trapped inside your body. Once this cover is off, it's only a matter of time until you notice just how positive and less racist your thoughts have become.

Question your negative beliefs and feelings.

- Always set your intention to release negative emotions related to race, before you do this exercise.

There are more than a few methods of getting to the subconscious root of an emotional state or belief. I use a technique that I call "Mind Probing." It involves questioning a conscious belief or feeling and then questioning the answer that you receive. You will then question the previous answer and then the answer after that and continue like this until you can't go any further.

Question your beliefs of the people you hate. Any negative thing that you believe about a particular race of people, take time to question this belief. Ask yourself, "why is this (the belief) a problem for me?'. Every answer you get, question that answer, keep questioning each following answer until it becomes uncomfortable for you. Don't stop there, keep going until the answers are more about you and less about the people you hate. The more uncomfortable the answer is the better. In fact, you should always give the most uncomfortable answer because these are usually the true answers. It's only uncomfortable because "the truth hurts."

To make it easier to pull out the best answers, do not repeat your answers and always give an answer. (Before you begin a session with this procedure, be sure to set an intention to "always give an answer and to only use each answer once).

Really commit to this idea because avoiding the truth is only defeating the purpose of this process. If you are trying to avoid the answers, you might as well have not begun the process in the first place.

In the spiritual community, this is a form of what is known as Shadow Work. I suggest that you find different methods of Shadow work to see what works best for you. Research it on the internet. You'll find good content in Shadow work on platforms like YouTube.

Find a life coach that does it or ask your therapist if they specialize in going into the subconscious.

Some people believe that even hypnotherapy can pull you to these subconscious aspects. Apply it to your racist beliefs to find the root truth of the beliefs. Try out anything that you believe could work. You'll be pleasantly surprise at how much help you can find and some of it is absolutely free.

Finding the basis of which the surface beliefs stands, helps to release a great deal of the emotions that is keeping you in this hatred.

You will find that 99% of the time, the root of your racist beliefs is very far from the topic of race. It will be closer related some deep-rooted fear that you have been carrying around since your childhood.

Once you have found this root belief you can now find ways to change that belief. I suggest you do an internet research on how to change a belief; there are people who specialize in the changing of negative beliefs.

How do you benefit from this "healing Stuff?"

You may not feel "super" interested in part-taking of these emotional exercises because maybe you are one of the many people who believe that racism doesn't negatively affect you as much as it does the "minority" groups. You may also feel like you are doing this healing for others and not you. But how sure are you that racism doesn't negatively affect you?

Even the people who are extremely rich, powerful and white are at the least, "annoyed" by a certain aspect of racism. Different People are affected in different ways.

All people are affected by racism if "one people" is affected, in the similar way as it works with "classism". E.g. If many people are poor, it creates criminal activity, which includes robbing and stealing from the rich. If there is an "underclass", it creates tension and animosity between that underclass and the upper class. So, both sides are affected.

Some white people don't regularly face discrimination because of their whiteness but some of these white people feel a sense of guilt and shame. They especially feel annoyed, guilty, and ashamed when they hear others speak of how their privilege may put non-whites at a disadvantage.

Isn't this painful for you as a white person? Wouldn't you prefer to live in a society where you don't have to live your life feeling the pain of white guilt and shame?

Working on yourself using the methods that I've provided in this book, will help to release this guilt and shame. This release will also serve to heal the world from racism.

How?

The guilt and shame that you carry manifests itself as more resentment and hate towards others. Think about it, why would you want to live and share a space with someone who makes you feel guilty or ashamed?

Even if we get the "race Baiters" to "shut up", this doesn't guarantee that all of them will go away. Shutting them up does not heal you. Your guilt/shame will still exist. So there will be instances where you will encounter someone who makes you uncomfortable with their race bating. When you are healed from the white guilt and the white shame, you will be comfortable whether they race bait or not.

Believe it or not, the guilt and shame create emotions and energy that leads to conflict (i.e. the war monger mentality).

Healing yourself is healing from the discomfort of this guilt and this shame. And your personal healing is your individual contribution to a Global problem. Your individual contribution counts just as your political vote, in an election.

So, you see, everyone has a valuable role to play here. There is no such thing as "Racism is not my problem" because if one demographic is affected, you can bet it will spill over unto you on some level and in some form, even if it's just discomfort.

Healing yourself = your contribution = your benefit. Everyone heals = everyone contributes = everyone benefits.

Tips and techniques on how to release negative feelings associated with racist beliefs.

Recognizing your emotions associated with racist beliefs and thoughts.

It amazes me how humans spend their whole lives feeling their own emotions, without consciously recognizing just how physical these emotions are. There is no way you could actually be reacting to things like fear and anger without some existing sensation inside of you that is a literal, physical feeling.

It seems like people perceive emotions the same way they perceive thoughts, they can't see or touch it, so therefore it's not that real. It is sad that I have to say this to you, but your emotions are physical. If you are in an uncomfortable emotional state, you are feeling something physical.

Another truth is, you are always in an emotional state. It's not possible to not feel an emotion in any moment. Even when you are in a very calm, "apathetic" state, you are feeling emotions. You are always feeling something.

That being said, you can use emotions in every moment as an opportunity to know where you are and where you stand regarding any matter in your life. This is good because once you can acknowledge these emotions, you are already ahead in your healing process.

The Three-Layer Release Method

I designed a technique to release negative emotions called the "Three-layer release Method." You will be releasing your racist feelings and emotions using this technique. You will be addressing, naming, and describing the emotions on three different energy levels. The Trigger level, the Emotion level, and then the Sensation level.

Whenever you see someone from a certain race that gives you negative feelings or triggers. Pay close attention to your entire body. Feel your body from head to toe, see how you feel, if you feel a trigger or a discomfort, acknowledge this first. Then speak to yourself, explaining everything in the moment that is causing you to be triggered by this person(s). Describe everything about that person and or their race and the current situation that troubles you.

Then at the Emotion level, you will have to name the emotions, I.e. anger, frustration, hatred, fear, insecurity, or whatever you are feeling.

Now here is where it gets a little complex. With the Sensation level you will try to recognize the exact sensation each feeling is giving you.

Each emotion has a particular sensation, for example, fear may feel like a warm/hot ball of boiling energy in your chest, a heavy hollow ball of gas in your stomach, a knot in your throat, a rush of heat in your limbs or other parts of the body.

When you start to feel the emotions of the racist/prejudice trigger, recognize each emotion and the sensations of it and call it out and describe them just like I did above.

Example 1:

You can do this full process like this: You can say these things aloud or silently.

- Always set your intention to release negative emotions related to race, before you do this exercise.

1. <u>The Trigger level.</u>

"There is a Black person." "I am having racist feelings and thoughts." "I can't stand that black person in my presence right now, I can't stand them in general". "I recognize that I feel uncomfortable because of seeing a Black person." "I want to run away." "I am panicking".

2. <u>The Emotion Level</u>.

"I feel anxious" (Anxiety).

3. <u>The sensation level.</u>

"This Anxiety feels like there is a soft electricity flowing all through my body with a big mass of oil in my stomach, it also feels like there is heat boiling in and around my upper body, a heavy aching bag of gel in the middle of my Torso".

While doing this observe what is happening to the sensations as you call them out, they should shift and change while becoming lighter as you go. This is how to know that you are starting to release them.

Keep in mind that anxiety, fear, and any emotion will feel different for different people, so be sure to state yours exactly how you feel them.

Keep naming the emotions and sensations until you feel a relief. You can repeat the process with the same emotion if you are not satisfied with the relief you feel from doing it once.

If you feel more than one emotion, call them out all at once (at the "emotion level") then describe the sensation of them individually. So, after you're done describing Anxiety, move on to insecurity, fear and the following ones that you have listed in that order.

When you are describing the sensations, you may feel a hesitation from not knowing how to really describe them. Sometimes they feel indescribable. Do not pressure yourself to get it right. Just use whatever word that closest, fit the nature of the emotion and feeling. Even if it means creating your own words for them. You would do this by letting your mouth follow the texture, sensation, and shape of the feeling.

This exercise works by you releasing the discomfort of the negative emotions, through your words. The idea is to continue describing all that you are feeling until you feel a relief.

Note: this will not bring you an immediate cure, but it relieves the discomfort in the moment and it can eventually bring long-term results after a while of doing it.

Example 2:

This process involves using your hands to locate the sensations.

Just like the previous method, you will be working with three different energy levels.

You will start out acknowledging the trigger, aloud or silently.

So, if you walk into a room with black people and you become uncomfortable and or triggered by their presence, this is a better method for you to do on spot because you don't have to use words, if you don't want to. It will go something like this:

<u>1. Trigger level.</u>

"Ok, there are black people in this room." "I am acknowledging that I am uncomfortable/triggered."

"I want to leave right now, I am panicking, and I feel like screaming, I feel like bursting, I can't stand this, I can't stand them".

At the trigger level, you need to acknowledge, all that you are thinking, believing and feeling even if it seems unkind and degrading. This is how you release the negative energy, by expressing it the way in which it does exists.

<u>2. Emotion level.</u>

"I feel frustrated, Angry, Anxious, fear. - (here I am demonstrating what I just suggested in example one; calling out more than one emotion and then describing them one at a time in the sensation level).

<u>3. Sensation level.</u>

Here you will locate each emotion with your hand, follow the feeling as it shifts with your hand while describing the feeling and describing the changes it is making as you follow it.

Use your fingers to point at the area in your body that you feel the sensation of frustration. If you feel it in your arms, point at it while describing the sensation to yourself silently (or aloud if you're alone). So, you can point at your arm and say, "this frustration, it feels like a tight clenching, warm energy, its swirling around as I speak, it feels like it's moving towards the left side of my chest." Keep following it with your hands and describing it, go wherever it goes until you feel strong relief.

Now move on to the next emotion; point at the area in your body that you feel the anger. If you feel most of it in your chest and upper abdomen, point at the area you feel it the strongest, if that's your chest, say: "this is anger, it feels like a huge hot eruption of airy fire that continues to blaze, it is calming as I point at it".

Anger is a very powerful state, so you may feel it in more than one or two different places in the body, so you may have to work with one area, then move on to the other after you're done.

Of course, stay with the feeling, following it and describe it as it moves until you feel it no more or until it is comfortable enough to go about your day.

I believe it's best to do these kinds of procedures exactly when the trigger is happening. It's hard to do them in public places, so if you can't do them then and there, I suggest you take at least three deep breaths to calm yourself in that moment. Take the breaths, in through your nose and out through your mouth; then set an intension to work on it later.

How do you work on it later? You will get home or just wait until you are in a comfortable place, by yourself. Now you will visualize the earlier scenario, when you were in that public place and you saw the people that caused that trigger. Then try to remember exactly how you felt at the time. Think about all the things that made you upset about the people at the time, and you can think about all the reasons why you hate those people in general.

The aim is to allow the memory and the thoughts to bring up the very emotions and feelings that you felt with the trigger. Then when you start to feel as much pain as you possibly can, use one of the "Three Layer Release methods" to work with the emotions that you brought up.

<u>Here is a much quicker and easier version of this same kind of self-work.</u>

- Always set your intention to release negative emotions related to race, before you do this exercise.

It's simply talking to each emotion for quick relief. This shouldn't take you more than one minute to do. You will be speaking to the feelings like they are a person.

When you encounter a situation where you feel Racist/prejudice thoughts and feelings creep up on you, just stand or sit still for about one minute and speak to the feelings themselves saying:

"You are my racist feelings, I see you, I understand you, I am here for you and I am giving the permission to exist".

You should use up the one minute carefully. I suggest that you take only fifteen seconds to just feel and acknowledge the feeling. Take another fifteen seconds to watch all that is going on in your body, just a quick scan of your body from head to toe, noticing all of the uncomfortable sensations. Now take the other 30 seconds speaking to the feelings, saying what I just told you to say.

If you are walking or just going about your day when you are triggered, you don't have to stop, you can just say it to yourself silently while doing what you are doing.

I suggest you do one of these, every time you see a person or people of other races, because you may think you are not having a "racist moment" when you actually are. Believe it or not, every time you see a person of another race, you get racist feelings. Every time you see someone of another race, one of the first things you think about is their race, you just don't realize it because it is mostly subconscious.

If you are having a problem with the idea of giving racist feelings "the permission to exist", please remember that the best way for healing is by feeding the negative energy with positive energy. So, giving the feelings permission to exist is a form of positive energy. Any other approach is a fight, and fighting is negative energy, which adds more negative energy to the racist feelings, which cause them to increase.

Other quick and easy ways to transform racist feelings

The "Small self" visualization technique

- Always set your intention to release negative emotions related to race, before you do this exercise.

The idea here, is for you to create a visual image for the feeling.

The way to do this is to use your mind to turn the sensation into a small version of yourself.

You would do this by feeling all that is occurring in your body. Then close your eyes and observe the sensation. Based on what the sensation feels like, you will create a visual image for it. The feeling can dictate the shape of the sensation. What I mean is; you will know what shape an object has based on how it feels.   It's just like when you step on a pen, you can tell the shape of what you are stepping on, because the feeling is long, straight, thin, and cylindrical against the bottom of your foot. This is how you can determine the shape of the emotional sensation in your body.

When you are around people who give you these racist feelings. See what part of your body has the strongest feelings. Close your eyes and observe the shape of the feeling, keep the image in your head until it becomes has clear and vivid as possible.

If the sensation is like a big mass of water, then see it as that, if it's more like electricity then see it as such, whatever it feels like or seem like just visualize it as that very image.

If you can't recognize the shape of it, just allow the feeling to be whatever it is.

Now use your mind to transform the present image into a small version of you. (While you are doing all of this, you may notice that the feeling itself is changing, don't let this stop you just continue to the next step). (Just acknowledge the changes and continue).

After you've changed it into a small version of you, I want you to visualize a small version of someone that you deem as supportive and loving to sit down with the small version of you, in the area of your body where the feeling is. This person can be a loving parent, any family member, or any person in your life that loves and care for you.

Have them sit together in conversation. Have the supportive person give the small "you" supportive words.

Have them say things like " You exist for a reason," "I am here with you now and forever"; "I am giving you the permission to exist." Have this loving person; continue saying these things until you feel a big relief or until you feel like stopping.

When you are done, express your gratitude to the loving person that helped you, and ask him/her to be there with your "small self" forever. Then you will take three deep breaths, open your eyes, and continue with your day.

Just know that this person is always there within you. You can always call on them whenever you get the uncomfortable racist feelings or any negative feeling and in any part of your body.

The spinning method

- Always set your intention to release negative emotions related to race, before you do this exercise.

Whenever you feel your racist feelings coming on, acknowledge them as your racist feelings, close your eyes, and scan your body for all of the sensations that are there. You can visualize while doing this or just choose to slowly spin the feelings in a clockwise direction with the intention to transform them into positive feelings and positive energy. Keep the spinning the images in your mind until you start to feel light and blissful, or until you feel satisfied. When you are pleased with what you feel, acknowledge how great you feel. Now take three deep cleansing breaths and then return back to your regular life.

Depending on how much bliss you want, this can last for one minute to twenty minutes.

The Drawing technique (drawing your racist emotions)

- Always set your intention to release negative emotions related to race, before you do this exercise.

When you feel your racist feelings creeping up on you; feel the emotional sensations in your body, choose to feel them, visualize them, and listen to them. Give them your undivided attention.

Get a pen and paper. Now, based on what they look and feel like, just start to draw them. You can do this by letting your hand use the pencil to follow the form of the sensations in your body. Follow them and if they move as you draw, follow to direction it takes with your pencil.

You can do this in sections, meaning, you can draw the energy in one body part at a time. Keep going until you feel a relief. You can do this as many times as needed.

The Experience reversal method

- Always set your intension to release negative emotions related to race, before you do this exercise.

You can use this visualization with just about any negative experience in your life, including personal experiences and even events that happened before you were born. If those events or the images of those events bother or upset you in anyway. These events can be anything that happened in life that you know about. They can be big events and small events. They can be things like Slavery or just something that occurred in life that you grew up hearing about.

However, this particular demonstration is pertaining to your personal experiences with people of other races (or the group that you dislike). You can do this one with recent personal experiences and also the ones you've had in the past.

It's the process of using your mind's visualizations and imagination to reverse an experience or event while impacting your emotional system.

The method that I will demonstrate here involves events that happen in your direct and personal reality relative to race/racism.

Example: If you went out and about, and you encounter a situation involving a person or people from the race or group that you dislike that was seriously devastating or just uncomfortable, I suggest that you acknowledge the unpleasant feelings from this experience while you are in that scene.

When you get home, I want you to sit down in an area where you won't be interrupted. Now try to remember the whole experience in the proper sequence. If you miss or forget a few details, its ok, just let it be, and just try to remember all that you can. Also, it's important to allow the memory of it to bring up the same negative feelings that you had while this was happening.

Follow it in your mind from start to finish. It's almost like you are re-living the experience in the exact order in which it happen.

When you get to the end of the experience in your mind, you are going to say to yourself silently, (or aloud), " I am about to recreate this experience/event in order to release the negative feelings that it caused.

Now try to rewind every detail that you can remember in the sequence of which it occurred. You will rewind it in your mind like a video cassette tape. (Remember to watch how the feelings and sensations in your body are reacting to this reverse action and acknowledge any change that is occurring).

Continue to rewind the experience in your mind until you get to the beginning of it and right before it even happened. At this point, acknowledge that you have totally reversed the entire experience and you just "undid" what was done. Now you are going to recreate the experience as a positive and pleasant one.

So, see yourself on that very scene with the people who did and or said something that upset you. You are now going to see them do or say something totally different.

Example if the actual experience was one in which a fight occurred involving a person or people of a certain race (which created or heightened your racist feelings), just recreate this scenario by seeing both individuals simply pass by each other and say hello, while continuing to walk away from each other. Visualize this happening and watch as they both vanish from the scene. Immediately after that, see yourself doing or having a very happy and pleasant experience. See yourself walking away from that area and meeting up with a loved one who brings a smile to your face. Alternatively, see yourself walk away to buy ice cream or your favorite meal or stepping in a building to hear your favorite song on the radio. Whatever you choose, make sure it is something that always bring you joy in your everyday life. Stay in that feeling of joy, enjoying that pleasant experience of the loved one, the meal, or the music until you feel great.

You can keep going with this pleasant feeling for as long as you want and when you are done, take three very deep breaths then go on with regular life.

This whole process can last anywhere from five minutes to as long as you want.

The details in writing may seem like a lot but once you start doing this, it really can be short and easy.

The importance of accepting your prejudice/racist thoughts and feelings.

Don't ever fight your feelings or thoughts. Whatever you fight is going to fight you back. Not only that but you will not win this fight. The reason why you will lose, is not because of the fight itself or because you are weak but because of the reason you believe you must fight.

The reason you believe you have to fight is because you believe you have already lost. If you know that you have won, then you would not have to fight.

Whenever someone wants to fight, it's because they believe that they are being defeated, which means that they are weaker or feel weaker than their opponents. And It goes without saying, that if you are fighting someone who is stronger than you, you will lose. The winner of any fight does not continue to fight because he has already won.

The same applies for the mind, the reason why people fight negative thoughts and feelings is because they believe that these negative thoughts and feelings have already won. In other words, it's because they feel powerless to their own negative thoughts and feelings.

Whatever you believe is, and will be true, so if you are fighting your feelings and thoughts by rejecting or resisting them, then they will win.

This means you will get thoughts and feelings that are even more negative and in this case, you will get more racist thoughts and feelings.

Anything you do and express to shun your racist feelings is a fight. Sometimes you are fighting your feelings without knowing that you are. You may think you know what a fight is, but you may not.

A fight will be anything you do to condemn, reject, or resist a thought, belief, emotion, or feeling. If you believe that what you are thinking, or feeling is wrong, you are fighting yourself.

When you are trying to be politically correct, you are fighting your feelings. When you get mad at yourself for having negative thoughts about people of another race, you are putting up a fight and like I said before, this will not take the negative feelings away, it will only increase it.

A simple way to manage your racist thoughts and feelings is to simply let them be. Let them happen. Let them be what they are.

A good way to do this is to use simple affirmations to remind yourself to let these thoughts be.

When you feel your racist thoughts or feelings come over you just silently say to yourself, "I am where I am". You can also say things like: "I am having these feelings, and I choose to let them be" or "this is me, feeling racist/prejudice, I choose to let these feelings exist".

By doing this you are doing two important things, you are acknowledging your feeling and then letting them go. This way you don't stay in a continuous conflict with yourself and so instead of the negative energy increasing they will go where you want them to go. You will eventually transform them into positive energy.

This is how you practice the art of acceptance. This is not just acceptance of your feelings; this is ultimately a form of self-acceptance. Your feelings and thoughts are aspects of you, so accepting them is accepting you. This kind of self-acceptance, also leads to accepting others.

Accepting your feelings reduces the discomfort you feel around other people and so you'll find it easier to accept these people.

This is especially true, because if you are constantly fighting your feelings towards a particular race of people, when you see them you will be 1. triggered and 2. Reminded that these are the people that are causing the discomfort from the conflict in your mind, which heightens the resentments towards that type of people.

So, starting to accept your feelings is one way to start accepting others.

Work for specific Races

I just provided a few healing techniques and methods that all races of people can do. However, specific groups need attention and self-work uniquely for themselves.

There are groups who see themselves as the victims and therefore see others as the perpetrator. There are others who are in a more powerful position that sees themselves as more valuable and the "less powerful" as second-class citizens.

It's important to address each group's problems separately because the beliefs that are responsible for their social problems are quite pervasive and is keeping us all stuck in a negative pattern.

Each race has at least one specific crutch that is a detriment to their own community without them even knowing it. I will speak only of two races regarding this matter.

Black people's number one issue is Victimhood and White people's number one issue is White entitlement. We have to work on releasing the beliefs and emotions that serve to maintain these two mindsets.

Most black people don't want to face the fact that victimhood is at the root of a lot their issues, complaints, concerns and experiences.

Most white people will say and do anything to dismiss the idea that they suffer from an unhealthy sense of entitlement relative to their whiteness.

If people don't learn to recognize these mental conditions within themselves, there will be no understanding and there will be no healing of the nation.

I believe the first step for black people to take right now towards building a stronger community is building a stronger mind that is free of victimhood. Black people have to start by re-programming their minds to see their own greatness and also eliminate the beliefs that creates low expectations.

One main reason why this is important is because whatever you focus on as an individual, you will create more of. So, whatever you focus on as a collective you will continue to create collectively.

Dwelling on something negative will cause people to focus on you negatively. So, if you dwell on your victimhood or take actions that stem from victimhood, people will pick up on it subconsciously and identify you as a victim.

For Example: So much of the rhetoric that comes with black people's victimhood, involves blaming whites. This blaming trigger an anger within whites that makes them want to attack. In this, Blacks are victimized even more.

If you are focusing on mostly negative things, then you will become mostly negative and you will attract more negativity. This works the same for people in groups.

If a common people believe the same negative things, they will collectively expect negative things and thus attract negative things as a group. You have to re-program your mind to see and expect better, richer living experiences.

<u>For Black People</u>

I am providing some mind shifting re-programming exercises for black people (and any person or group that sees themselves as oppressed).

If you consider yourself as being a part of a minority group, then these exercises are for you as well.

- These techniques might seem simple or ineffective at first, but you have to know that re-programming your mind is not as complex as you may think. Try them.

Again, whatever you focus on you create more of. If your life is mostly horrible this is because you have been focusing on everything that makes it horrible. You get blinded towards the things that are good in your life and so your perception cannot get pass the negatives to see the positives.

No matter how bad things are in your life, there has to be some good, even if it's just the good weather or having your favorite meal sometimes. If you take note of even the smallest positive things in your life, it helps to shift your consciousness towards positivity and thus attract less negativity.

This works for you as an individual and this will work for black people collectively if we get many black people practicing this positive focus. This will help to keep you away from most of the pain and trials involved with racism.

Long story short: Even if things are bad, find the things that are good and continuously focus on them and you will attract more good than bad.

Positively focus on your community

People who focus on positive things, thinks and believe positive things. They will radiate a positive vibe and so people will gravitate towards them, treat them and give them that same positive vibe; what you put out, people will give back to you. This works the same in a negative way. People will treat you the way you treat them, and people will, at times, treat you the way you treat yourself.

Right now, your mind is packed with negative thoughts about your community. The more you continue to think like this the more you will see, expect, and thus attract bad things for your community.

When you search for the evidence of positivity in your community and in your people, you will start to attract more of these positive things and positivity in general.

- Make a list of all the negative issues in your community that needs work. Then beside each one. Write down at least three reasons why you can be hopeful that it will get better.

- Always set your intention to release negative emotions related to victimhood, before you do this exercise.

For example: If the first thing on your list is "We have very little job opportunities." You can oppose this belief by saying, this can get better because:

1. "The economy may be improving."

2. My people are becoming more "woke" now and this may help them to come together in some ways that may lead to us building and creating resources.

3. We have an increasing amount of people creating businesses for themselves, so it seems like things are slowly becoming better.

Remember this is a list, so write down as many problems as possible with at least three positive opposing statements. Even if you don't have the strongest faith in the positive opposing statements, write them anyway, because any amount of faith is good to help to create a different mindset from the one you currently hold.

This is what's most important, to write just about anything that will make you feel better. The better you feel the more positive thoughts you will generate and therefore create positive life experiences.

Do not go off thinking that you are doing this only for yourself. Your positive energy will positively affect your community, as you should share this kind of thinking with everyone you come across and soon the collective reality for the people will be affected.

- Make a list of how and why your community is doing well.
- Always set your intention to release negative emotions related to victimhood, before you do this exercise.

You may not think that your community is doing great overall, but the idea is to search for any detail that suggest positivity and positive occurrences in the community. So, write down the very big victories and the very small things like watching someone holding the door for another person. Just search for anything that will restore your faith in your community and your people.

Example:

1. The Sports industry is dominated by black people.
2. The music industry is dominated by black people.
3. More black people are attending college these days.
4. The number of Black business owners is growing.
5. There are more black billionaires now more than ever before.
6. Black people are waking up more to a higher consciousness more and more.
7. Black people are becoming more spiritual.

When you can't find anymore-big things now you could start adding the smaller things. These things can be as small as the little things you see going on in your neighborhood, school, and church or even in your home. For example:

1. Today, I saw that they were cleaning up and renovating the Arts and cultural center in my (black) neighborhood.
2. There are four black owned stores in my neighborhood.
3. I know a couple people who have their own black hair care business.

This list was my list. You must create your own list that is specific to you and your life. Some of the items on my list will also be on your list because we live in the same world, but you should know best which applies to your life or not. Please do not lie or write false information on this list or any of these mind-reprogramming exercises because lying will not be effective at all.

You may notice that I wrote items related to money and some that aren't related to money, its best to make your list just the same. Make sure whatever you write is true and only makes you feel good.

- Make a list of progresses that the Black community
  has made throughout history.

- Always set your intention to release negative emotions related to victimhood, before you do this exercise.

Example:

1. A Black man invented the Traffic Light. (You can add as many Black inventions to the list as you'll like).
2. We actually had a Black President.
3. Many cities in the country have black mayors.
4. More black filmmakers are going mainstream in Hollywood.

* Make this list as long as you can. Use points from my example list, only if it applies to your life. Read them over as often as possible.

- Make a list of why black people today aren't victims.

- Always set your intension to release negative emotions related to victimhood, before you do this exercise.

Example:

1. Because the amount of black people who are victims of police brutality is a small compared to the number of black people in the country.
2. Because physical Slavery ended a long time ago and does not exist in my country today. (if slavery exists in your country then don't write this one in your list. Try to focus on your direct "black" reality).

3. Because most black people walk the streets every day and make it home safely.
4. Because most black people today aren't being physically harassed by racists.
5. Because there are many rich black people in the world.
6. Because most black people in the world have some level of freedom.

* Make this list as long as you can. Use points from my example list, only if it applies to your life. Read them over as often as possible.

If you notice, in this list I tried to not lie to myself about the realities of the world as it relates to black people's plight. I use the word "most" and not "all" in reference to black people today, because there are some people who do and have experienced racial victimization. So, I am not invalidating their experiences but at the same time I am not focused on the negatives because the aim of these exercises is to reprogram my mind by focusing on the good that does exist instead of the bad.

Because the truth is the victimization of black people are not happening to most black people, even though it is happening to some.

You are not doing this to be selfish or to disregard the unfortunate events but instead to create a positive outlook for yourself and so you'll attract positive experiences as an individual. This is why it is extremely important for all black people to do this mind re-programming because if each individual should change their victimhood mindset then the community as a whole will create a different reality by using this new positive energy to stave off racism and racial crimes.

- Make a list of how black people are living in Prosperity Today.

- Always set your intension to release negative emotions related to victimhood, before you do this exercise.

Examples:

1. The Black music industry brings in billions of dollars every year.
2. We have more than one Black billionaire.
3. We have more Black millionaires living today than ever before.
4. The number of Black business owners is climbing.

You can also write a list like this, stating the local success in your neighborhood, community, and family.

* Make this list as long as you can. Use points from my example list, only if it applies to your life. Read them over as often as possible.

- Make a list of the beauties of being black. Both, the inner and outer beauty of blackness.

Example:

- Always set your intention to release negative emotions related to victimhood, before you do this exercise.

1. Black people are very spiritual.
2. Black people are very artistically creative.
3. Dark skin means more protection from the sun.
4. Black hair is capable of taking on many different hair styles.
5. Chocolate skin has a beautiful glow.
6. Black people are very family oriented.

* Make this list as long as you can. Use points from my example list, only if it applies to your life. Read them over as often as possible.

You can make it into a two-column list to separate the inner beauties from the outer beauties.

Try to only write the things that you truly believe are beautiful. If there are things about blackness that you don't find desirable, do not put it on this list. When you write down the things you truly adore, it registers more to your brain because the brain knows it's the truth.

~ I have a couple of mind and emotional exercises that may be considered controversial, but I suggest that we all should consider them.

One of them is to make a list of the positive aspects of racism. Meaning you can think up all the good things that exist because of racism. A list like this will mostly be consist of lessons learned from bad experiences.

Everything negative that we experience in our lives is serving a higher purpose. It is here to teach us about ourselves and our relationship with others and the Universe at large; it's up to you to find all the inherent lessons involved in any bad situation.

For example, you can write things like:

1. Racism cause black people to come together in certain ways.
2. Racism causes us to understand to importance of unity.
3. Racism taught me certain things about the human mind.

* Make this list as long as you can. Use points from my example list, only if it applies to your life. Read them over as often as possible.

With this list, you can write down as many lessons you've learned and any positives that you believe came from racism. Please only write down positive things, do not write anything egotistical or related to revenge or anything like that.

So, do not write things like: "Racism taught me who my enemies are," or "Racism makes me want to go out and kill," or things like "racism taught me the White man is the devil".

This kind of thinking will only defeat the purpose of the idea of "positive focus." This will not help you in anyway; it will only cause you to attract more negativity.

- Try to find any reasons why your "enemies" may have some good inside of them.

Some people in the black community will find this kind of thinking to be problematic because they perceive it as "kissing ass."

You as a black person is not doing this for "your enemy," you are doing it for you. You are doing this to put yourself in a better emotional and vibrational position where you can begin to create a heathy community.

The health starts first on a mental emotional level. As long as you continue to hold others accountable for your pain, you will never be able to create peace because you will expect them to do something to fix your pain and that is impossible, because they can't even fix their own pain.

In addition, you will always be fighting the pain within ourselves and of course, whatever you fight, will fight you and win.

The frustration of having to fight the inner fight will extend to the creation of the bigger fight between you and your "enemies" which will never end and will eventually lead into bloodshed and war.

If Black people do not learn how to let go of the pain that exist for them because of things like slavery, it will ultimately lead to them attracting slavery again.

Here are some examples of the things you can put on this list:

1. My "enemies" are good because they are humans like me and I'm good, so they must have some good in them.

2. Because if they were all bad then life probably would have been worse.

3. Because only a portion of them commit horrible "hate crimes" now.

    Write as many as you can think up.

*   Make this list as long as you can. Use points from my example list, only if it applies to your life. Read them over as often as possible.

This is not for you to lie to yourself, be truthful about this.   Please only write down the things about your "enemies" that you truly believe makes them good people.

This is for you to keep a positive outlook even on the negatives. When you keep your mind focused negatively on the negatives, you will attract more of these negative experiences and occurrences. When you find ways to shed a positive light on the bad things, these things will have a less impact on your mind and body.

"If you change the way you look at things, the things you look at change." - Dr. Wayne Dyer

<u>Try to keep an "attitude of gratitude."</u>

- Always set your intention to release negative emotions related to victimhood, before you do this exercise.

Keep a special journal, specifically for writing down all the things in your life that you are grateful for in your life. Also try to write a gratitude list every day. Write about all the good things that happened in your day that you are thankful for. Write anything good, from the smallest things to the biggest things. If you get a raise at your job, give thanks for it in your journal and if you were driving home and you saw that the sunset made you feel good, give thanks for it in your journal.

Its best to write in this gratitude journal right before bed. This way you will sleep happy and awake happy.

When you are in a thankful spirit, you radiate a very high positive energy that will attract mostly positive experiences. And so, you as a black person can attract a better life for yourself.

This will also help your mind to believe that there is and can be "more good" in life than bad. It's best to be truthful about your gratitude. Do not write the things that you are forcing yourself to be thankful about or the things others thinks you should be thankful for. Only write the things that make you "light up" when you think of them, because this is true gratitude.

Again, what you believe is true, so true gratitude will create "more good" in your life and more things to be thankful for.

<u>Prayer and Meditation</u>

Your beliefs about the effectiveness of meditation does not objectively define meditation. It has been proven time and time again that meditation helps to create a different energy force around you and therefore a different life. It does this by calming and quieting the mind.

Quieting the mind puts you in a state where you are stopping all the negative thoughts to make way for positive thoughts. Positive thoughts create a positive life.

Meditation can help to clear your mind of the negative thoughts that expects racist occurrences (be sure to set the intention for this). The less you expect negative things to happen the more you will live a happier life and the more you will be inspired to show others how to have higher expectations from meditating.

<u>Use your prayer to heal yourself and the world</u>.

Most people do not expect prayer and meditation to help in healing racism for two reasons. 1. They have been praying for centuries about the problems of the world but sometimes it seems as if it's only getting worse. 2. Because they believe that only the government can do something to solve racism. This is telling me that very few people know the value of putting in an intention in their prayer.

Start dedicating some of your prayers and meditation towards the problem of racism. So, do at least one meditation and prayer related to your personal prejudice and fears related to racism.

All you have to do is set the intention before you pray or meditate to release your own prejudices towards others.

Say this: I am setting my intension for this prayer (or this meditation) to release any prejudice or racist feelings that I have towards "others."

Then when you're in prayer just pray about everything that is bothering you about race issues in society. Also pray about how a particular race makes you feel in every way. Whomever or whatever you pray to, tell them about the emotions you feel when you start to experience your prejudices. Ask your God to heal you of these feelings.

Tell your God about the state of current politics related to race relations in the society. Ask him to help you to trust that the state of the world will change and of course continue to tell him about everything else that you are concerned with in your life.

At the end of the prayer, express your gratitude about the healing that the prayer will bring.

This particular method may not be for everyone as not everyone is religious, but a lot of black people are religious and thus will have a lot of faith in prayer.

You don't have to pray to any known religious deity, you can just decide to say a prayer to life itself or to the Universe. It's not about whom or what you are praying to, it's about trusting that sending and requesting positive energy outwards will put you and your mind in a positive state.

The reason prayer works is because of the intention and faith involved with prayer.

Understanding and Benefitting from this Self Work.

You have to trust that when you start to think more positively about your life, you will start to attract more of these positive things. Some people will argue that this approach is way too passive, and it will not work. But the truth is most of the times when people are using aggression to fight the system, their problems increase for two main reasons. 1. Aggression is an extension of fear, so the thoughts related to the aggressive actions you are taking will only manifest more of the same problem.

2. As I may have said before, whatever you fight will fight you and win. If you are fighting the system, it's because you believe that you have already lost the battle. This is the root belief of why you are fighting. Your root beliefs are your true beliefs and so you will only manifest more of the truth.

Specifically, for white people

White people and black people share the same physical world, while living two separate realities. Their social/political status, culture, history, norms have created different lives for them, along with certain inherent aspect of the human psyche, personality and nature. These things also cause both people to expect different things.

If you're a white person who was born to parents, who were also born to parents that lived in a time where their "whiteness" gave them a certain advantage over others, then a very strong sense of entitlement will become a mental state for you and people in the White community.

Even in today's world, this sense of White entitlement still exists because White parents have been sending indirect and subconscious messages to their children that denotes white entitlement.

This transfer for information is subconscious and unconscious which is why most white people living today don't know that they still believe in and exude White entitlement.

The era of Political correctness and tolerance training has convinced white people's conscious minds that they no longer think this way.

This unawareness of white entitlement, along with white people living and being concerned with their own lives has cause them to only be able to understand life from their perspective.

Meaning, most of them don't understand the concept of White supremacy, White privilege, or White entitlement.

Whites live their lives with the hardships and "easy-ships" of being white; they only know how to expect things that come at them at their level. All they see is all they know and all they know is all they see. They cannot see or understand that black people aren't expecting the same things because they can only see and live what they are used to.

What blacks may see as white entitlement, white people see as just their normal way of thinking and expecting.

<u>What are the factors that created the mind state of White entitlement?</u>

In history, the systemic structure of racism sought to make the White race, the superior race. The supporters of this concept went out of their way to use psychological warfare on the masses to program both whites and non-whites of this lie. Whites were given special treatment as a result.

The special treatment, the idea that they are the majority, the belief of them having higher intellect, the fact that they have done many inventions and the building of governments and states, the fact that they generally live a higher standard of life. Along with the idea that these things are the standards of which everyone should measure their worth, has been some of what has shaped this sense of entitlement for White people.

The "White status" consciously and subconsciously tell whites that they are advanced beings and therefore more deserving of everything that life has to offer. Almost as if God is more in favor of them than other Humans.

So many other unconscious, subliminal programming are set in place to alter the human mind in buying into the belief that "White" is special.

I am not going to list all the contributing factors that help to build this paradigm, but there are a few things that I have notice that is very hidden and subtle.

I believe the words we use in reference of different racial groups can help to shape the perception of a race in relation to the other(s).

Take for example, the word Minority. This word has a specific meaning. In definition, it means that some people are less in numbers than others, but I believe the context in which we use it today in regard to race, has a very demeaning connotation to it.

We use it to describe people who aren't white, which suggests that white people are larger in number than other people. Now maybe white people are in fact larger in numbers but using this word as a definite label for non-whites has always set a tone. It always feels like it is somehow synonymous with the word inferior.

You don't have to tell me the real meaning of the word "minority." I'm just simply saying that regardless of the true definition, it sets a different tone that suggests inferiority and I'm sure most people feel this, they just aren't highly conscious of it.

The term "mainstream America" is used to describe White society in America. This is another word that has a meaning but eventually send a subliminal message of White people being bigger than others. It sets white people apart from others and sends the message that whites are "normal" and non-whites are "other." It sends a subliminal message that Whites are more special and it helps to maintain this sense of entitlement among Whites.

If I were not able to make you as a white person, believe in the validity of your White entitlement, I still ask that you challenge yourself to the following procedures. Just try them out to see how you'll feel afterwards. These are actually simple methods of mind re-programming.

- Make a list of how black people and other "minorities" are not a threat to your "whiteness" and the White community.

- Always set your intention to release negative emotions related to race, before you do this exercise.

Example:

1. Most black people are just trying to live their lives without hurting anyone.
2. Most of the times when I see black people, they never try to hurt or harass me.
3. The people in the black community that do bad things are the minority.
4. The white people who date non-whites are the minority

* Make this list as long as you can. Use points from my example list, only if it applies to your life. Read them over as often as possible.

Even if you do perceive these people as a threat to the white community, just try to search for any possible way in which they are not a threat.

- Make a list of why you and other White people are good people.

- Always set your intention to release negative emotions related to white entitlement, before you do this exercise.

Example:

1. Most people in my family are white and are kind loving beings.
2. I am white, and I know within my heart that I am a good person.
3. If White people weren't good then the whole world would have been destroyed already.
4. Because there are good and bad people in every race.
5. I have not done anything to physically harm anyone of any other race.

* Make this list as long as you can. Use points from my example list, only if it applies to your life. Read them over as often as possible.

- Make a list of why it's not a bad thing to be White.

  ▪ Always set your intention to release negative emotions related to white entitlement, before you do this exercise.

Example:

1. I was born white and it's not my fault.
2. Because White people are humans like everyone else.
3. Because "God" made me, so I must be good.
4. Because there are good and bad people in every race.

Do not write anything that may be belittling, degrading or negative towards other groups of people. And do not write anything that is arrogant or egotistical towards yourself.

You may think putting others down will make you feel powerful but in this case it will not. In fact, it will do the opposite. On the surface, it may seem like power but the root of it, which is the truth of it, is actually pure weakness.

* Make this list as long as you can. Use points from my example list, only if it applies to your life. Read them over as often as possible.

- Make a list of why there will always be enough resources for all races of people to share.

  ▪ Always set your intention to release negative emotions related to white entitlement, before you do this exercise.

Example:

1. Because we live on a large Planet with so much of everything.
2. Because there is so much money in the world.
3. Because there is an abundance of soil to grow foods everywhere.
4. Because there is limitless oxygen for us to share.
5. Because "God" wouldn't put us all here if "he" knew there wouldn't be enough.
6. Because we have been using up resources on the earth or thousands of years now and it keeps providing.

* Make this list as long as you can. Use points from my example list, only if it applies to your life. Read them over as often as possible.

- Make a list of why you as a White individual will always be important regardless of how diverse your country become.

  ▪ Always set your intention to release negative emotions related to white entitlement, before you do this exercise.

Example:

I am important as a white individual regardless of diversity because:

1. Because I am important to the people in my family.
2. Because no one can be me but me.
3. Because I contribute to the greatness of this country.
4. Because I am an independent person that lives for himself.
5. I have an Education.
6. I have a Trade.

* Make this list as long as you can. Use points from my example list, only if it applies to your life. Read them over as often as possible.

- Make lists of the ways in which each Minority group has, does, and will contribute to the progress of the country. (If you want, you can make 1 list for each group/race).

  ▪ Always set your intension to release negative emotions related to white entitlement, before you do this exercise.

Example: You can write it like this.

How have Black people contributed to the progress of our country?

1. They have a lucrative market in music.
2. The sports industry is also lucrative.
3. There are Students from Africa who are doing very well in the country.

* Make this list as long as you can. Use points from my example list, only if it applies to your life. Read them over as often as possible.

Make Meditation a Practice.

Do at least one every week. To understand more about Meditations, do an online research. There are hundreds of different kinds of free meditations on YouTube. Try Meditations that is designed to silent the mind. You may find that you begin to think more positively about your own life and the people you share this world with.

So, what about the browns?

Every now and then, I hear people complaining, saying that society only care about two races when it comes to racism. They say we only care about White people and Black people, while ignoring that there are others between them.

There are a few reasons why Black people and White people remain the two most focused upon groups when it comes to racism.

1. Black people and white people have spent much more time in either physical conflict or silent conflict with each other.
2. They are at the extreme ends of racial/social politics.
3. One group is very accepted by most and the other group is the opposite.
4. One experience wealth while the other experience many different levels of poverty.

The people who are non-black/non-white have prejudices and are racist too. So, I am not leaving you guys out. Take the following approach to your own feelings of racial prejudice and social politics.

If you don't know which techniques to use for your healing. Try to see what side you most identify with, Black people or white people. If you see eye to eye and or empathize more with white people, then do the exercises designed for everyone and the ones that are specifically for white people.

If you identify as a minority or some of your social issues are similar to those of black people, then practice the techniques that are intended for everyone and also the ones that are especially for black people.

Why will people commit to these Procedures and why will they work?

You may think, "Most people will never commit to these methods of healing; therefore, life will never get better." You may be right, but I am optimistic because of three reasons.

1. If People have always collectively commit to being Politically Correct for such a long time then they can collectively commit to healing their nation and their world. This time using methods that actually will work.

2. I have enough faith in my work and I know just how ground breaking my material is. This kind of teaching is the type that truly resonates with people because it represents the aspect of them that most other systems are not addressing when it comes to racism, i.e. the subconscious mind.

3. People will be willing to try something fresh and different, especially since we are all so very desperate and hungry for real solutions. People will be willing to test this all out to see what works.

Many people will not take time to do the work that I present in this chapter, out of reluctance, laziness or from the belief that they don't have to because racism is not their problem.

If you've found that you are one of these people, its ok. I would only ask you to keep the memory of the philosophies of this book. I would also ask you to be mindful of the points that I presented as "Things to Consider." Even just these things can help to shift your consciousness to a fresh new outlook on race and how it affects your life. Even doing these things can contribute to a societal change.

Things to remember when doing these procedures

Do not rush the process of progress

You don't have to do all these techniques and exercises at once. Take your time. Once you've set the intention to heal, your being will listen to the Intention and take you where you want to be.

Depending on who you are and just how committed you are to your healing, you may find that you want to commit to one or two of my techniques per week or month. You can choose a couple or few that works for you and continue to use them until your mind and or body feels like it could move on to other techniques.

You will know when you're ready to move on based on the fact that you'll feel that the ones you are currently using aren't working as strongly anymore. Or maybe you'll just get tired of using them. Either way this is an indication for you to try something different or new.

~~~~*

<u>You will benefit in many ways</u>

These Emotional healing practices will help you to heal in areas that are not just related to your racism. You may notice that other aspects of your life seem to be running smoother. It's because all of your negative emotions are connected, and you have multiple issues that stem from the same trauma. So, healing the pain related to your racist feelings can extend to other hurt feelings that you have been carrying around in your life.

You may start to work on releasing your racist feelings and notice that you suddenly became more confident in doing certain things that you were always afraid of doing e.g. maybe you were a guy who use to have a big fear of approaching women, and after a while of working on your racist feelings, you realize that you've develop a certain amount of confidence and bravery to approach women.

<u>Be Patient</u>

Stop expecting sudden healing and just know that you are not a bad person for having these racist feelings and you will be in much better place, soon. The desire to become better is a way to know that you are a good person. Having racist thoughts and feelings does not make you bad or evil. It makes you Human, and every Human has a dark side and within the darkness lives negative beliefs about every aspect of being human including race.

<u>Giving Positive Energy to Negative Energy</u>

Your life is unpleasant right now because it is true that there are bad things happening in our world and bad things do happen to good people. However, it is also very true that your life is especially unpleasant because of the things you are focused on.

Have you ever noticed that once you start thinking negatively, you tend to keep thinking negatively? This is because like attract like. You think one negative thought and it attracts another and then that one attracts another, and then another until your mind and emotional system is overflowing with negativity.

You should know that this is how your life experiences work too, because when your mind is filled with negative thoughts, it is going to be directed towards the things in your reality that are just as negative. It will only see, notice, highlight and expect the negative related things.

You also attract negative experiences the same way, because the more you expect bad things the more you will pull them towards you.

This is why it is important that all people use these focus exercises to program their minds to see and expect positive things relative to race relations, because when the majority of humans shift their minds to believe and expect more positive experiences, our collective reality has to change. The world has to become a safer place for everyone because our minds are now synced on one path of positivity.

Giving positive energy to your thoughts, beliefs, and feelings is like giving positive energy to anything in your life. It most likely will create positive results. Fighting or suppressing your negative/painful feelings and beliefs will only create more of the same.

If you see two people fighting, you won't end the fight by joining the fight. You end you fight by breaking it up.

The fight is negative energy and the breaking up of the fight is positive love energy. The kind of energy you apply to anything is the same kind of energy it will manifest.

Giving positive energy to your racist feelings is how to create an internal integration. There has to be an internal integration in order for a social integration to happen. If you are fighting yourself, you will be fighting others. You cannot be at odds with yourself and be at peace with other people.

You have to trust that when you start to think more positively about your life, you will start to attract more of these positive things.

Some people will argue that this approach is way too soft, and it will not work. But the truth is most of the times when people are using aggression to fight the system, their problems increase for two main reasons.

1. Aggression is an extension of fear, so the thoughts related to the aggressive actions you are taking will only manifest more of the same problem.

2. As I may have said before, whatever you fight will fight you and win. If you are fighting the system, it's because you believe that you have already lost the battle. This is the root belief of why you are fighting. Your root beliefs are your true beliefs and so you will only manifest more of the truth.

What If?

What if the things we see as inferior, are not inferiorities but rather, just differences. What if the "lowest" form of living is not low but just a different way to live; and the people who live this "low" life are not "low-lives" but just a different kind of people. What if Black people are different from White people for a reason?

I do know that we are all one, but I would be lying if I said that I didn't notice the differences between the races. It seems to me that black people and white people are built differently in certain aspects, be it mentally, emotionally, spiritually and obviously physically. White people have always had their own way of being that comes with certain interests.

Black people seem to carry an essence that tends to be more in line with being free spirited and expressive. I believe that this is an inherent state that extends to even genetics and I also believe that the uniqueness of each race is here to serve a higher purpose.

In a perfect world, Black people's unique qualities would be just unique and that would be ok.

We don't live in a perfect world. The world we live in has been operating with a consciousness that supports a very narrow way of perceiving and thinking.

Uniqueness and differences are sometimes perceived as inferiorities and flaws and so the initial response to black people's nature was one of condemnation and rejection.

Once White people started to condemn black people's uniqueness and perceive them as inferiorities, they acted on this perception. They "treated" black people as inferior beings, which is abuse. Abuse lead to deep emotional trauma which created dysfunction and despair within the black community.

This dysfunction has traveled through the centuries and through the generations. It creates an even stronger perception of inferiority that leads to even more abuse, and more abuse means more trauma and more dysfunction. And now non-blacks are convinced that black people are either cursed and or inherently inferior.

What we don't realize is that black people's natural way of being uniquely free spirited, was seen as a degenerate flaw because free spirited-ness within itself is perceived as disorder to begin with. Now add this free-spirited-ness to "dysfunction" (from abuse) and now this is a sure recipe for perceived inferiority.

Some whites, non-blacks and even some black people clutch on to the belief that blacks are inferior because it serves their egos to see others as less than them. So even the people who know that this perceived black inferiority is a lie, wants it to be true.

In this Universe, all is one and all is connected. This ultimately means that every living thing is of equal importance in the eyes of the Universe (God).

We humans have the perception of high v/s low, big v/s small, important v/s unimportant due to the concept of identity (ego).

When we use identity to define ourselves we create a strong need for hierarchy and this inevitably leads to suffering because one group has to subdue the other to maintain this system of hierarchy.

THE RACIST WORKSHEET

The Racist Worksheet, represents one aspect of the acknowledgement stage of healing from our racist feelings.

It is designed for the purpose of releasing trapped emotional energies related to your racist feelings.

The feelings that have been stuck in your system from years of suppression of your truth, due to living in a politically correct society.

I recommend that all people complete this worksheet, being that all of us are racist to an extent.

You can write up one of these worksheets at any time and regarding any race or group of people. You can do it as many time with the same race. But I do recommend that you do it at least once regarding the race of people that bothers you the most.

Please make copies of the racist worksheet for yourself and for your friends, families, associates and others.

On the next page I will be explaining the worksheet in the order in which it works. The next step will be the sample copy of the worksheet, showing you how you can fill it out.

Then after that are copies of the worksheet itself.

THE RACIST WORKSHEET

Understanding the Worksheet.

* **The Admission Stage**

This worksheet is built in different stages. Each stage is a progression of the previous.

It is designed this way to gradually release each layer of the racist energies within your emotional system.

The admission stage is the acknowledgement stage is the stage where you will be acknowledging the truth of the existence of your racist feelings.

* **The Three Level Emotional release stage**

I like to coach people using a three-aspect rule, I address the emotional system on three levels.

1. The Trigger Level
2. The Emotion Level
3. The Sensation Level

This is a very powerful way to ensure that negative energy is being released from your body and from all angles.

1. The trigger Level.

List and explain the things you are thinking and believing, when you see the races of people who bother you. Here you are going to also explain the urges you get and the things you feel like doing in the moments when you see or think about the races that triggers you.

2. The emotion Level.

At this level, you are simply going to list all the emotions that you feel when you see or think about the object of your trigger.

3. The sensation Level.

Describing the physical sensations of the emotions that you listed in the Emotion level. You will observe the physicality of the emotions and try to put it in words. If you can't find a word to describe them, just make up your own words. Just make sure the word you make matches the feel and form of the sensation. It doesn't have to sound like any known, normal language and it doesn't have to make sense. Just say the word that pops in your mind and forms on your tongue.

THE "RACIST" WORKSHEET

(Sample)

This is a sample sheet on how the "Racist Worksheet" should be completed.

*   **The Admission Stage**

* I Mark Jacobs_ is a _Racist_. (<---write the word Racist here)

* I am Racist towards _Black people_.

* The first time I felt racist feelings towards _black people_ was _about 27 years ago when I was 9 years old.

* I was taught to be racist towards black people by my mother.

*   **The Three Level Emotional Release Stage**

1. The Trigger Level.

Please write in the best and honest answers.

Example:

* When I see _black people_ I think thoughts like _"they are going to rob me"_, "they are not very smart_".

* I may Stereotype them as "being fatherless_" and Disorderly and "as criminals".

* When I see _black people_, I get the urge to _run away.

* When I see _Black people_, I want _to leave the area to only be around white people.

* When I see __Black people_ I want them to __go away forever_

2. The Emotion Level.

List all the emotions that you feel when you see or think about the object of your trigger.

Example:

* When I see _black people_ I feel __frightened_
* When I see _black people_ I feel __fear_
* When I see _black people_ I feel __angry_

3. The sensation level.

Describe the sensation of each emotion listed above.

Example:

* When I feel _frightened_ from seeing __black people_, it feels like _a hot/icy blow to my heart area, and an electric tingling in my arms_.
* When I feel__fear_from seeing _black people_, it feels like a hot ball is sinking in my chest, plus a rush of heat throughout my whole body_.
* When I feel _angry_ from seeing _black people_, it feels like there is a raging fire in my stomach, arms, and legs.

- Now always finish this exercise saying this:

"These feelings a true, these feelings are real, and these feelings are valid, so I choose to accept these feelings for what they are".

<u>THE RACIST WORKSHEET</u>

Always set your intention to release negative emotions related to race, before you do this exercise.

Say to yourself: "I am setting my intension to use this exercise to release any negative emotions/feelings related to race/racism."

The admission Stage

* I _________________ is a _________________ (Racist)
* I am Racist towards _________________________________
* The First time I felt racist feelings towards __________ was ____
* I was taught to be racist by ______________________

The three-level emotional release stage.

Below please fill in the blanks, stating what you feel like doing and the actions you feel like taking when you see the race of people that bothers you.

1. The Trigger level

* When I see _________________, I think thoughts like ___________, I also think thoughts like_____________
* When I see _________________, I stereotype them as _________________ and _________________, and ____
* When I see _____________________, I get the urge to ____

* When I see ______________________________, I want to ____

2. The Emotion level.

At this level, you are simply going to list the emotions that you feel when you see or think of the race of people that bothers you.

* When I see ________________, I feel ________________
* When I see ________________, I feel ________________
* When I see ________________, I feel ________________

3. The sensation level.

At this level, you will describe the physical sensations of the emotions that you listed in the Emotion level.

* When I feel ____________ from seeing ____________,
it feels like: ________________________________
* When I feel ________________________ from seeing
______________ it feels like: ________________
* When I feel ________________________ from seeing
______________ it feels like: ________________

-Now always finish this exercise saying this:

"These feelings are true, these feelings are real, and these feelings are valid, so I choose to accept these feelings for what they are".

<u>THE RACIST WORKSHEET</u>

Always set your intention to release negative emotions related to race, before you do this exercise.

Say to yourself: "I am setting my intension to use this exercise to release any negative emotions/feelings related to race/racism."

The admission Stage

* I _________________ is a _________________ (Racist)
* I am Racist towards _________________________________
* The First time I felt racist feelings towards __________ was ____
* I was taught to be racist by ____________________________

The three-level emotional release stage.

Below please fill in the blanks, stating what you feel like doing and the actions you feel like taking when you see the race of people that bothers you.

1. The Trigger level

* When I see _______________, I think thoughts like _____________, I also think thoughts like_____________
* When I see _________________, I stereotype them as _______________ and _________________, and
  ____
* When I see __________________, I get the urge to
  ____

* When I see _________________________________, I want to

____

2. The Emotion level.

At this level, you are simply going to list the emotions that you feel when you see or think of the race of people that bothers you.

* When I see ________________, I feel ____________________
* When I see ________________, I feel ____________________
* When I see ________________, I feel ____________________

3. The sensation level.

At this level, you will describe the physical sensations of the emotions that you listed in the Emotion level.

* When I feel ______________ from seeing ______________,
  it feels like: ____
* When I feel ___________________________ from seeing
  ______________ it feels like: __________________________
* When I feel ___________________________ from seeing
  ________________ it feels like: ________________________

-Now always finish this exercise saying this:

"These feelings are true, these feelings are real, and these feelings are valid, so I choose to accept these feelings for what they are".

THE RACIST WORKSHEET

Always set your intention to release negative emotions related to race, before you do this exercise.

Say to yourself: "I am setting my intension to use this exercise to release any negative emotions/feelings related to race/racism."

The admission Stage

* I _________________ is a _________________ (Racist)
* I am Racist towards _________________________________
* The First time I felt racist feelings towards ___________ was ____
* I was taught to be racist by _______________________

The three-level emotional release stage.

Below please fill in the blanks, stating what you feel like doing and the actions you feel like taking when you see the race of people that bothers you.

1. The Trigger level

* When I see _________________, I think thoughts like _____________, I also think thoughts like____________
* When I see _________________, I stereotype them as _________________ and _________________, and

  ____
* When I see ___________________________, I get the urge to

  ____

* When I see ________________________________, I want to

____

2. The Emotion level.

At this level, you are simply going to list the emotions that you feel when you see or think of the race of people that bothers you.

* When I see ________________, I feel ____________________
* When I see ________________, I feel ____________________
* When I see ________________, I feel ____________________

3. The sensation level.

At this level, you will describe the physical sensations of the emotions that you listed in the Emotion level.

* When I feel ____________ from seeing ____________,
it feels like: ____
* When I feel ________________________________ from seeing
________________ it feels like: ____________________________
* When I feel ________________________________ from seeing
________________ it feels like: ____________________________

-Now always finish this exercise saying this:

"These feelings are true, these feelings are real, and these feelings are valid, so I choose to accept these feelings for what they are".

<u>THE RACIST WORKSHEET</u>

Always set your intention to release negative emotions related to race, before you do this exercise.

Say to yourself: "I am setting my intension to use this exercise to release any negative emotions/feelings related to race/racism."

The admission Stage

* I ___________________ is a _________________ (Racist)
* I am Racist towards ____
* The First time I felt racist feelings towards ____________ was ____
* I was taught to be racist by ___________________________

The three-level emotional release stage.

Below please fill in the blanks, stating what you feel like doing and the actions you feel like taking when you see the race of people that bothers you.

1. The Trigger level

* When I see _________________, I think thoughts like _____________, I also think thoughts like_____________
* When I see _________________, I stereotype them as _________________ and _________________, and ____
* When I see ___________________________, I get the urge to ____

* When I see _______________________________, I want to

____

2. The Emotion level.

At this level, you are simply going to list the emotions that you feel when you see or think of the race of people that bothers you.

* When I see _________________, I feel __________________
* When I see _________________, I feel __________________
* When I see _________________, I feel __________________

3. The sensation level.

At this level, you will describe the physical sensations of the emotions that you listed in the Emotion level.

* When I feel _____________ from seeing _____________, it feels like: _______________________________________
* When I feel _________________________________ from seeing _______________ it feels like: _______________________
* When I feel _________________________________ from seeing _______________ it feels like: __________________

-Now always finish this exercise saying this:

"These feelings are true, these feelings are real, and these feelings are valid, so I choose to accept these feelings for what they are".

<u>THE RACIST WORKSHEET</u>

Always set your intention to release negative emotions related to race, before you do this exercise.

Say to yourself: "I am setting my intension to use this exercise to release any negative emotions/feelings related to race/racism."

The admission Stage

* I _________________ is a _________________ (Racist)
* I am Racist towards _________________________________
* The First time I felt racist feelings towards ___________ was ____
* I was taught to be racist by _______________________

The three-level emotional release stage.

Below please fill in the blanks, stating what you feel like doing and the actions you feel like taking when you see the race of people that bothers you.

1. The Trigger level

* When I see _______________, I think thoughts like _____________, I also think thoughts like_____________
* When I see _______________, I stereotype them as _______________ and _______________, and
  ____
* When I see _________________, I get the urge to
  ____

* When I see ____________________________, I want to

____

2. The Emotion level.

At this level, you are simply going to list the emotions that you feel when you see or think of the race of people that bothers you.

* When I see _______________, I feel ________________
* When I see _______________, I feel ________________
* When I see _______________, I feel ________________

3. The sensation level.

At this level, you will describe the physical sensations of the emotions that you listed in the Emotion level.

* When I feel _____________ from seeing ____________,
  it feels like: __________________________________
* When I feel _________________________ from seeing
  _____________ it feels like: ____________________
* When I feel _________________________ from seeing
  _________________ it feels like: ________________

-Now always finish this exercise saying this:

"These feelings are true, these feelings are real, and these feelings are valid, so I choose to accept these feelings for what they are".

<u>THE RACIST WORKSHEET</u>

Always set your intention to release negative emotions related to race, before you do this exercise.

Say to yourself: "I am setting my intension to use this exercise to release any negative emotions/feelings related to race/racism."

The admission Stage

* I ___________________ is a ___________________ (Racist)
* I am Racist towards ___________________
* The First time I felt racist feelings towards __________ was ___________________
* I was taught to be racist by ___________________

The three-level emotional release stage.

Below please fill in the blanks, stating what you feel like doing and the actions you feel like taking when you see the race of people that bothers you.

1. The Trigger level

* When I see ___________________, I think thoughts like ___________________, I also think thoughts like___________________
* When I see ___________________, I stereotype them as ___________________ and ___________________, and ___________________
* When I see ___________________, I get the urge to ___________________

* When I see _________________________________, I want to

____

2. The Emotion level.

At this level, you are simply going to list the emotions that you feel when you see or think of the race of people that bothers you.

* When I see ________________, I feel _________________
* When I see ________________, I feel _________________
* When I see ________________, I feel _________________

3. The sensation level.

At this level, you will describe the physical sensations of the emotions that you listed in the Emotion level.

* When I feel ____________ from seeing ____________,
it feels like: ___________________________________

* When I feel _________________________ from seeing
_____________ it feels like: ___________________________

* When I feel _________________________ from seeing
_________________ it feels like: _______________________

-Now always finish this exercise saying this:

"These feelings are true, these feelings are real, and these feelings are valid, so I choose to accept these feelings for what they are".

<u>THE RACIST WORKSHEET</u>

Always set your intention to release negative emotions related to race, before you do this exercise.

Say to yourself: "I am setting my intension to use this exercise to release any negative emotions/feelings related to race/racism."

The admission Stage

* I _________________ is a _________________ (Racist)
* I am Racist towards _________________________________
* The First time I felt racist feelings towards ___________ was ____
* I was taught to be racist by _______________________

The three-level emotional release stage.

Below please fill in the blanks, stating what you feel like doing and the actions you feel like taking when you see the race of people that bothers you.

1. The Trigger level

* When I see _________________, I think thoughts like _____________, I also think thoughts like_____________
* When I see _________________, I stereotype them as _________________ and _________________, and
  ____
* When I see ______________________, I get the urge to
  ____

* When I see _________________________________, I want to

____

2. The Emotion level.

At this level, you are simply going to list the emotions that you feel when you see or think of the race of people that bothers you.

* When I see ________________, I feel __________________
* When I see ________________, I feel __________________
* When I see ________________, I feel __________________

3. The sensation level.

At this level, you will describe the physical sensations of the emotions that you listed in the Emotion level.

* When I feel ______________ from seeing ____________,
  it feels like: ______________________________________
* When I feel _________________________ from seeing
  ______________ it feels like: _______________________
* When I feel _________________________ from seeing
  ________________ it feels like: _____________________

-Now always finish this exercise saying this:

"These feelings are true, these feelings are real, and these feelings are valid, so I choose to accept these feelings for what they are".

<u>THE RACIST WORKSHEET</u>

Always set your intention to release negative emotions related to race, before you do this exercise.

Say to yourself: "I am setting my intension to use this exercise to release any negative emotions/feelings related to race/racism."

The admission Stage

* I ________________ is a _______________ (Racist)
* I am Racist towards ___________________________
* The First time I felt racist feelings towards ___________ was ___________________________________
* I was taught to be racist by ___________________

The three-level emotional release stage.

Below please fill in the blanks, stating what you feel like doing and the actions you feel like taking when you see the race of people that bothers you.

1. The Trigger level

* When I see ________________, I think thoughts like ____________, I also think thoughts like_____________
* When I see ________________, I stereotype them as _______________ and ________________, and ____
* When I see ___________________, I get the urge to ____

* When I see _________________________________, I want to

____

2. The Emotion level.

At this level, you are simply going to list the emotions that you feel when you see or think of the race of people that bothers you.

* When I see _________________, I feel _____________________
* When I see _________________, I feel _____________________
* When I see _________________, I feel _____________________

3. The sensation level.

At this level, you will describe the physical sensations of the emotions that you listed in the Emotion level.

* When I feel _______________ from seeing _______________,
  it feels like: ____
* When I feel ___________________________ from seeing
  _______________ it feels like: _______________________
* When I feel ___________________________ from seeing
  _______________ it feels like: _______________________

-Now always finish this exercise saying this:

"These feelings are true, these feelings are real, and these feelings are valid, so I choose to accept these feelings for what they are".

THE RACIST WORKSHEET

Always set your intention to release negative emotions related to race, before you do this exercise.

Say to yourself: "I am setting my intension to use this exercise to release any negative emotions/feelings related to race/racism."

The admission Stage

* I _________________ is a _________________ (Racist)
* I am Racist towards _________________________________
* The First time I felt racist feelings towards __________ was _________________________________
* I was taught to be racist by _________________________

The three-level emotional release stage.

Below please fill in the blanks, stating what you feel like doing and the actions you feel like taking when you see the race of people that bothers you.

1. The Trigger level

* When I see _________________, I think thoughts like _________________, I also think thoughts like_________________
* When I see _________________, I stereotype them as _________________ and _________________, and _________________________________
* When I see _________________________, I get the urge to _________________________________

* When I see _________________________________, I want to

____

2. The Emotion level.

At this level, you are simply going to list the emotions that you feel when you see or think of the race of people that bothers you.

* When I see __________________, I feel __________________
* When I see __________________, I feel __________________
* When I see __________________, I feel __________________

3. The sensation level.

At this level, you will describe the physical sensations of the emotions that you listed in the Emotion level.

* When I feel _______________ from seeing _____________,
it feels like: ____
* When I feel _________________________________ from seeing
_______________ it feels like: _________________________
* When I feel _________________________________ from seeing
_________________ it feels like: _______________________

-Now always finish this exercise saying this:

"These feelings are true, these feelings are real, and these feelings are valid, so I choose to accept these feelings for what they are".

THE RACIST WORKSHEET

Always set your intention to release negative emotions related to race, before you do this exercise.

Say to yourself: "I am setting my intension to use this exercise to release any negative emotions/feelings related to race/racism."

The admission Stage

* I ___________________ is a _________________ (Racist)
* I am Racist towards _______________________________
* The First time I felt racist feelings towards __________ was ____
* I was taught to be racist by _______________________

The three-level emotional release stage.

Below please fill in the blanks, stating what you feel like doing and the actions you feel like taking when you see the race of people that bothers you.

1. The Trigger level

* When I see ________________, I think thoughts like ______________, I also think thoughts like____________
* When I see ________________, I stereotype them as ________________ and _________________, and

  ____
* When I see __________________, I get the urge to

  ____

* When I see ____________________________, I want to

____

2. The Emotion level.

At this level, you are simply going to list the emotions that you feel when you see or think of the race of people that bothers you.

* When I see _________________, I feel _________________
* When I see _________________, I feel _________________
* When I see _________________, I feel _________________

3. The sensation level.

At this level, you will describe the physical sensations of the emotions that you listed in the Emotion level.

* When I feel _____________ from seeing _____________,
it feels like: _______________________________________

* When I feel _______________________________ from seeing
_______________ it feels like: _______________________

* When I feel _______________________________ from seeing
_______________ it feels like: _______________________

-Now always finish this exercise saying this:

"These feelings are true, these feelings are real, and these feelings are valid, so I choose to accept these feelings for what they are".

ABOUT THE AUTHOR

Jada Aleesha is a Spiritual Intuitive. Her Intuition serves as a teaching center that brought her profound understanding about the many emotional trials that she had to battle throughout her life.

Her life was a series of bad events that taught her so much about her own mind and an understanding of the root of all her pain.

With this understanding, she was able to gain much awareness about the human condition, regarding many subjects, one of which is racism.

As a black child, born in a majority black country, she observed how the Black people were affected by White supremacy in a similar yet different way than it affects the Black people in a majority white country.

She migrated to the U.S. in her late teens and she got exposed to a whole different environment with a different culture and people.

Jada watched how racism in America, spiraled from being covert and subtle into a massive social divide and a new Era of overt White Nationalism and "Alt-right-ism."

Jada applied the wisdom that she gained from her higher intuitive state to the global problem that is racism. She made many discoveries that directed her on a path of knowledge that gave birth to the philosophies and reasoning in this book.

Follow Jada Aleesha at:

Websites: www.jadaaleesha.com/

Blog: www.jadaaleesha.com/blogs/

Coaching: www.lifecoachinfortlauderdalefl.com/

www.instagram.com/jadaaleesha_emotional_coach/

www.facebook.com/JadaAleesha/